George Poveromo's
SALTWATER
STRATEGIES & TACTICS

Published by
OUTDOOR ASSOCIATES, INC.
Parkland, Florida

PRINTED IN THE UNITED STATES OF AMERICA
ISBN 0-9706599-3-8

TABLE OF CONTENTS

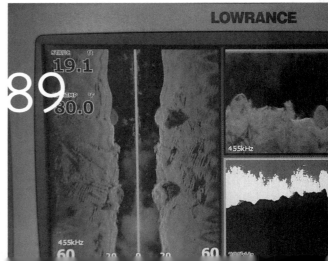

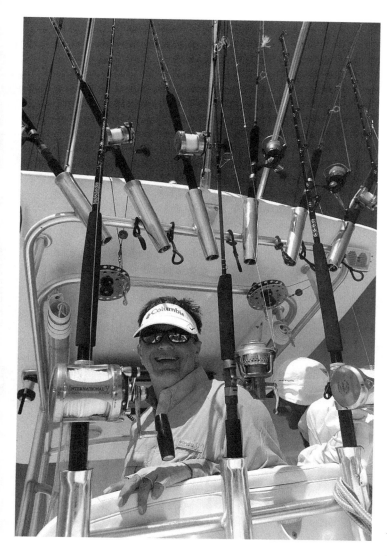

ABOUT THE AUTHOR

George Poveromo is a renowned angling authority who serves as Editor-At-Large for Salt Water Sportsman Magazine, the nation's oldest and largest publication on the sport of marine fishing. Considered the fishing authority for over 73 years, Salt Water Sportsman has a paid monthly circulation of over 150,000 readers. George has been on the publication's masthead since 1983.

George's in-depth knowledge of marine angling is the result of a lifelong passion for fishing. In 1983 he was recognized by Motor Boating and Sailing as one of the top eight anglers in the country - at age 23! He has fished along the entire U.S. coast, as well as in Alaska, Hawaii, Bermuda, Grand Canary Island, the Caribbean and a number of Central and South American destinations. His numerous feature articles in Salt Water Sportsman reflect his extensive background and expertise in salt water fishing, and his "Tactics & Tackle" column ranks among readers as the number-one department in the magazine. All of this has made George a household name among Salt Water Sportsman readers and members of the fishing and marine industries.

George is also well-known as the producer and host of the immensely popular Salt Water Sportsman National Seminar Series, the nation's largest and most successful educational course on recreational marine fishing techniques. Now into its 25th consecutive year, the National Seminar Series is an institution in the salt water sport fishing community. The tour visits eight major cities annually, and has educated over 130,000 anglers since its inception in 1988.

And if that's not enough to keep him busy, George is the producer and host of the immensely popular, nationally televised series *George Poveromo's World of Saltwater Fishing*. Through his hit television show, which has been airing for 12 years now, George teaches viewers how to catch a wide variety of game fish, from exotic species like blue marlin and bonefish to regional favorites such as dolphin, wahoo, tuna, king mackerel, striped bass, grouper, snapper, bluefish, redfish, flounder and numerous others. Filming occurs along the coastal U.S. and popular angling destinations abroad, and George is usually chasing the big ones down aboard his Mako 284 center console, MARC VI. A graduate of the University of Miami, he makes his home in Parkland, Florida.

Special thanks to Marcy Mock for her hard work in readying this book for publication.
marseadesign@mac.com

Special thanks to Donna Tasselmyer, for her eagle eyes in proofing this book
Special thanks to Greg Poland, Kevin Tierney, for use of some of their images

Chapter 1
7 Common-Sense Tackle Care Tips
Proper care adds years to your tackle and dollars to your wallet

Salt water anglers invest a small fortune (and many of us even "staggering" ones!) in fishing tackle, more specifically on rods and reels. Surprisingly, just a small percentage will go the extra mile and provide the TLC these outfits need to perform flawlessly season after season. Given the price tags on some of the more sophisticated reels and rods, I'm at awe when I see such gear banging against the gunwales of a boat, getting doused with saltwater, being improperly washed and stored, and even still spooled up with old and compromised fishing line.

Below is a tackle care "hit list" I adhere to, whether I'm crossing to the Bahamas, or chasing inshore game fish a couple miles from the boat ramp. If these tips are practiced, you'll gain peace of mind in knowing you're tackle will remain in perfect shape, and ready for anything a trophy class fish can dish out.

Scrub-A-Dub-Dub

How to properly wash a reel at the end of the day has always made for a great debate. That being said, the late Dean Hicks – a former tackle shop and reel repair center owner in Ft. Myers, Florida, took such a chore personally. "Dean O", as he was affectionately called, had cleaned and repaired thousands of reels in his day, and had come up with a "bullet proof" technique of cleaning and caring for reels.

According to Dean O, never use of any kind of pressure when rinsing reels, like aiming a hose or spray nozzle directly at a reel; this could force salt, sand and other elements into the reel. Instead he recommended a simple and very light freshwater rinsing at the end of each fishing trip. This goes for the rods, guides and reel seats as well. After rinsing and drying a reel, Dean O was a proponent of applying a light coat of lubricant to the reel and its components. And since many such products can break down the properties of fishing line, he had his three favorites: Super Slick's Slick Stuff, Reel Magic, and Corrosion X. Although with the latter, he advised using this sparingly and with great care, as it could damage some reel finishes and rubber seals.

One final tip on rinsing reels: Advance their drags – especially on spinning reels – which will further prevent water from seeping into these systems. It's also wise to hold a spinning reel upside down (drag toward the ground) when rinsing, giving water even less of an opportunity to invade the reel. Then, when the reels have been dried and wiped down with a lubricant, back off their drags and store the outfits.

Gunwale Rod No-Nos

Running through rough seas with outfits in above gunwale holders is among one of the worst things for your reels – particularly if they're drenched with saltwater on each big wave. Granted, quality offshore reels are made to withstand this type of abuse, but why press the issue? It only stands to reason that if a reel is drenched continuously over a considerable period of time (like a four hour run to a canyon), some salt will find its way into the system.

If above gunwale rod holders are all you have, that's one thing. But at least move the outfits from the boat's "wet" side to any under-the-gunwale racks, or, at the very least, use reel covers to shield the spray.

And for those trailer boaters: don't tow with your rods in topside gunwale holders, as I've heard far too many stories about fishermen getting their rods ripped off the boat - while stopped at a traffic light! Think about it: Such outfits are easy pickings for an on foot thief, or one in a car heading in the opposite direction (I've heard both accounts). And what are you going to do about it? Make a sharp U-turn with your rig and give pursuit?!

Under-The-Gunwales

This is the predominant rod storage area on a lot of small and mid size boats. When I set forth for an extended trip to the Bahamas, where I take a lot of different outfits, I'll rack the heavier (trolling) gear under-the-gunwales. By doing so, I'll have only the lighter spinning and conventional outfits in my T-Top holders, which puts little, if any, stress up there.

I'll make sure when racking rods under-the-gunwales to do so where the reels won't bang against each other. Ditto for the rods. I'll use a towel or a sponge to "cushion" the reels on these long runs, so they won't rub and vibrate – or even bang- against the boat. It's the same for their rods. Protective reel covers also offer excellent protection here.

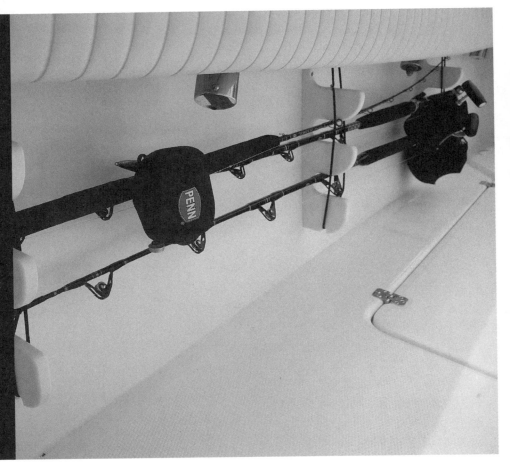

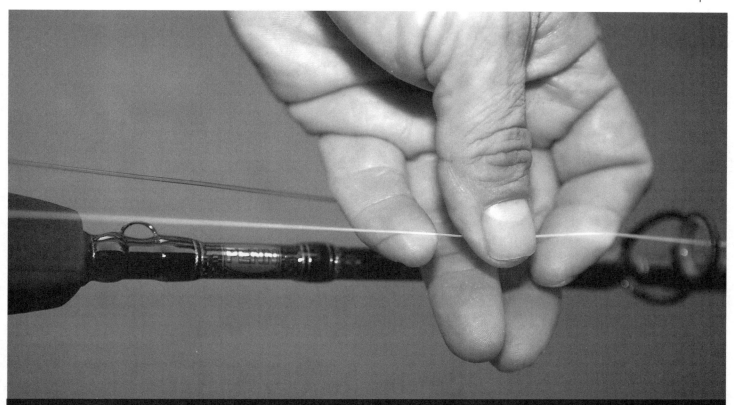

Best "Pickup" Lines

As a general rule, I replace my fishing line after any long, stressful encounter with a powerful fish. That's because the properties of the line were likely compromised during the bout. Outside of that, I monitor the "spin finish" on the line, which gives it its sheen. Once that begins to fade and the line isn't feeling as supple as when it was new, I'll change it out. Like maintaining a reel, keeping your fishing line fresh is critical to your success. A worn line might do just fine when bailing small school fish only to fail on a large, powerful fish.

Doctor's Appointment

Another item open to debate is how often to service a reel. Just because an angler plunks down $ 500.00 for a quality trolling reel, for example, that doesn't mean the reel never has to be serviced. If you purchased a $ 50,000.00 SUV to trailer your boat, would you assume because you paid that much that the vehicle would never need an oil change or servicing? Quite the contrary. You would go to all lengths to protect that investment. Why should your reels be any different?

As a rule of thumb, a reel should be brought to an authorized reel repair center at least once a year, and perhaps twice if those reels are under heavy duty usage – like on busy charter boats. This should entail a full overhaul, cleaning and lubrication.

Hey, Watch Those Rods!

Given the highly sensitive and ultra strong composite rods which are fast-gaining in popularity, and even those old reliable standard fiberglass ones, extra care should be taken to prevent damaging these blanks. I don't mean like rolling them up in a car window or slamming shut a car door on them, but rather something as unapparent as having a jig vibrate or bang against the rod blank while running to and from the fishing grounds. Little things like this, along with the way rods are racked (outlined above), make a big difference in their life span, or lack thereof.

For example, let's say we have a bucktail jig secured to the guide frame on a graphite or other "sensitive" composite rod. During the run to the fishing grounds, in bumpy seas, the jig vibrates and frequently "taps" the rod blank. Unaware to the naked eye, it is feasible that the rod blank now has a minute knick in it, from the jig. If that knick isn't along a critical spot on the rod, chances are nothing will happen to it. However, if the heat is put to a big fish, and that knick is indeed along a "pressure" spot on the rod, the blank can literally snap.

Therefore, when securing jigs, lures and hooks, avoid the rod guides entirely. Rather, affix them to the reel seat, or hook attachment points that manufacturers are now designing onto the reel seats, and even onto rod fore grips. And to make certain a jig, lure or hook remains tightly secured, wrap the fishing line two or three times around the rod and guides. This tactic should prevent it from loosening up during transit.

Stow Them Smartly

One of the best and least utilized tackle care items are rod bungees. In my opinion, these should be standard equipment on all new boats sold with T-Top-based rod holders. Rod bungees serve two main purposes. They will prevent a rod from launching from a T-Top holder when running in rough seas — and possibly injuring someone if it falls into the cockpit, or costing you a minimum of a few hundred dollars if it goes overboard.

All it takes is for one big wave and a little extra speed to launch your boat into the air. And that's when a rod or two will likely get pitched from their holders. The other advantage of rod bungees is that they keep their outfits tightly fastened to their holders, where they are less susceptible to vibrating and bouncing around, which could loosen screws and also beat up reels and reel seats.

It takes me about two seconds to secure the assigned bungee to each T-Top outfit. And when we reach the fishing grounds, I simply remove the bungees and make the rods readily accessible.

Chapter 2
Proper Fish Venting
Doing it right is an easy and effective way to release bottomfish

This story is my "ace of fins," the card I play when anyone suggests that venting a fish does more harm than good.

As the facts go, we were bottomfishing near Bimini, Bahamas, in 70 feet of water when I landed a 12-pound red grouper. The fish's swim bladder had expanded, virtually guaranteeing the grouper's death if it was released as is. Minus a venting tool (this was 15 years ago), I laid the fish upon a wet towel placed on the gunwale. I slightly punctured the rise in the flesh just aft of its pectoral fin with the end of the point of a thin fillet knife, expelled the trapped gasses from its swim bladder and released the fish. It swam slowly for bottom, seemingly none the worse for wear. This was confirmed by the underwater videographer, who was shooting the action for a bottomfishing video.

Four months later, we returned to the same numbers and caught the

Proper venting of an undersize or unwanted bottom fish which has experienced rapid decompression is essential to its survival. Pictured here is a Tiger Grouper.

same grouper, easily identifiable by the light venting scar. I repeated the procedure and returned the fish to the ocean. And if that wasn't coincidence enough, I caught the same fish the next time I fished that spot. Once again I vented and released it.

After that, I never saw that red

grouper again, leaving me to wonder if it ultimately ended up in someone's cooler, moved from that section of reef or died. Yet the bottom line remains the same: That fish had three opportunities to thrive and spawn over the course of eight months due to my venting it. There is little doubt about its fate had it not been vented: It would have wallowed at the surface and become an easy meal for a predator or died and floated away with the current.

To Poke or Not to Poke?

Whether venting a fish is beneficial or harmful stirs much debate. There's no denying that it can be stressful and sometimes fatal to a fish if done incorrectly. That's why, after you acquire enough fish for a few dinners, it's always sound practice to leave a bottomfishing spot or alter your tactics to catch fish at or near the surface. Yet even when food fishing, you are likely to catch undersize, undesirable or protected bottom species, which must be returned to the sea, before you limit out. And when these fish are reeled up from depths greater than 50 feet, the likelihood of swim bladder expansion and rupture — referred to as rapid decompression — is high. This is when venting becomes a viable option.

It should be noted that venting is required by law in Gulf of Mexico waters should an unwanted bottomfish come up bloated or have difficulty swimming back down. Though it is yet to be law along the rest of the coastal United States, it is often a sound choice. Off the West Coast, recompression is the preferred tactic. This involves returning a fish safely to the depths via weights so the increasing pressures recompress the gasses in the expanded bladder.

The Good Doctor

Dr. Karen Burns, Gulf of Mexico Fishery Management Council ecosystems management specialist, says reef fish rapidly brought up from depths of 50 feet or more are vulnerable to the expansion

Amberjack are susceptible to rapid decompression, when taken at depths greater than 50 feet.

of the gasses within their swim bladders. Many times these swim bladders burst, and the escaping and expanding gasses fill the fish's body cavities. Burns explains that reef fish such as red grouper, red snapper and vermilion snapper can experience swim bladder rupture beginning at 33 feet (the equivalent of one atmosphere). When a fish is on the bottom, the pressures associated with depth compress the gasses so they fit in its swim bladder. As a bottomfish is rapidly brought up from the deep, the

decrease in pressure allows the gasses to expand. As Burns points out, decompression when a fish is coming up leads to swim bladder expansion and rupturing. Rapid decompression is evidenced by the stomach protruding from a fish's mouth, the intestines protruding from a fish's anus or the bloating of the area behind a fish's pectoral fins.

Venting is especially effective on reef fish, like groupers, snappers and sea bass, which have large swim bladders. These are true bottom dwellers and the most vulner-

Proper venting of an undersize or unwanted bottom fish which has experienced rapid decompression is essential to its survival, as is working with the fish until it's strong enough to swim on its own - as is illustrated by this amberjack.

able to bladder expansion. Other species with smaller, thicker swim bladders can traverse the water column with less threat of barotrauma, and others with no swim bladders at all, like sharks, swordfish, cobia and mackerel, are immune to the problem. This is why they can dive deep during a fight and swim back to the surface with no apparent ill effects.

Just Venting

It's essential to execute the venting process as quickly as possible, with minimal handling of the fish. For example, when we bring up a grouper, snapper or amberjack from depths greater than 50 feet and wish to release it, we'll look for signs of rapid decompression. If the fish looks fine, we'll grasp its lower jaw, return it to the water and resuscitate it. If it appears to flounder at this stage and act like it may have problems going down, we'll vent it. To vent a fish, we soak a beach towel in salt water, spread it on the gunwale or cooler, and lay the fish on top. With one person holding the fish's head and tail, the free deckhand

will lay the pec fin flush against the fish's body. About an inch or so behind that fin, we'll insert a hollow venting needle on a slight angle and just deep enough to purge the gasses from the swim bladder — it sounds like we're letting air from a bicycle tire. It's critical not to insert the needle straight in or too deeply, which can damage a vital organ. As the gasses leave the fish, we'll begin adding slight finger pressure on the now deflating area to help compress the bladder and expel the gasses.

We then cradle the fish and put it back into the water, holding the lower jaw into the current so the water moving past the anchored boat flows over and through the fish's gills. If the fish was captured drifting, we put a motor into gear to generate water flow. Once the fish appears rejuvenated (tail kicking, jaw clamping down on hand), we set it free. We use this tactic commonly for grouper, snapper and amberjack. For large fish, like goliath grouper, we execute the venting procedure with the fish in the water.

If a released fish doesn't swim down, we'll get it back to the boat and work with it some more. If a fish was brought up from cool, deep water to hot surface water, it could be thermal stress and not improper venting causing the problem.

Venting Websites

These educational websites go into great detail about venting fishes.

www.flseagrant.org

www.catchandrelease.org

www.fishsmart.org

Venting Tools and Dehookers

ARC Dehooker

www.dehooker4arc.com

Alien Products SnapperSaver

www.snappersaver.com

Team Marine USA Dehooker

www.teammarineusa.us

Ohero Vent For Life

www.oherofishing.com/www.ventforlife.com

Proper venting of an undersize or unwanted bottom fish which has experienced rapid decompression is essential to its survival, as is working with the fish until it's strong enough to swim on its own - as is illustrated by this amberjack.

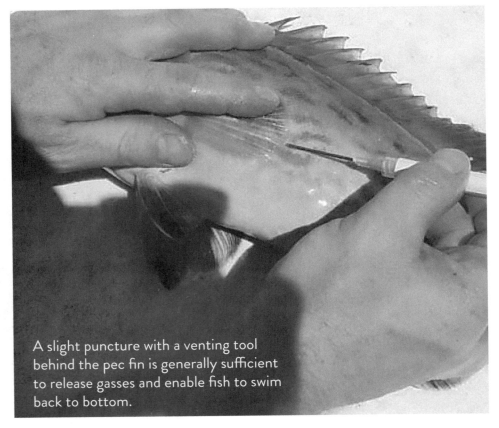

A slight puncture with a venting tool behind the pec fin is generally sufficient to release gasses and enable fish to swim back to bottom.

The Right Stuff

Tools of the trade include a hypodermic or other hollow, well-honed, tiny-diameter and thin-walled stainless-steel needle. Knife and hook points are not recommended. The tool should be hollow for the gasses to escape. And make absolutely certain to clear that channel of flesh and scales. Do this by rinsing the tool in alcohol or bleach, drying it and then blowing through it. After it's cleaned and checked, put the cap over the tool and store it in a safe yet easy to access place. Remember, time is of the essence when removing a fish from the water and venting it, and it can't wait for you to clear a clogged needle.

Venting is a good, quick means of helping unwanted bottomfish get back to their lairs with a good survival rate. Yes, there will always be those who question the value of venting, but I will always go back to my red grouper story as proof that venting does indeed work — and is a much better option than setting unwanted fish afloat to die. ✳

The SeaQualizer is easy to use and has proved incredibly effective for releasing bottom fish.

Chapter 3
The SeaQualizer
An innovative new device promises improved deep water releases

The anticipation built as we closed in on a bottom spot some 84 miles out in the Gulf of Mexico off Sarasota, Florida. It wasn't just the flutter-jigging action we hoped to find that fueled our excitement, but the opportunity to test a brand-new release device for bottomfish, one which could render venting obsolete. Little did I know just how easy and effective this device would prove on the red snapper and undersize red grouper we were about to catch.

Releasing undersize, unwanted or closed-season bottomfish is a daunting task, and for good reason. When benthic species such as groupers, snappers, sea bass and tilefish are brought up from depths of 50 feet and more, their swim bladders expand due to the reduction of pressure, which com-presses internal gasses, as the fish ascend in the water column. Expanding gasses enlarge swim bladders and can in extreme cases force them to rupture. Damage from pressure change is known as barotrauma and results in fish that are bloated, primarily around the pectoral fins. Their stomachs may protrude from their mouths, and intestines from their anuses. So unless a released fish is properly vented — that is, has its swim bladder punctured with a needle — it won't be able to return to its lair. It will die or become forage for a larger predator.

With venting, a hollow needle is inserted into the pectoral region of a bloated fish to penetrate the swim bladder and release the gasses, which allows the fish to swim back to the bottom. While venting has proven to be successful, it is not without contro-versy. Many people, including some from the scientific community, think venting actually harms fish and isn't as effective as we'd like to think in preserving a fish's life. Of course, there's the other side, which says that without venting, fish have zero chance of survival. Many think that if venting is done properly and no internal organs are punctured, fish survive just fine and the slight puncture wound from the needle or venting tool heals.

The SeaQualizer Revolution
The device I tried off Sarasota is the SeaQualizer, a tool for safely and efficiently releasing bottomfish back to their environment. It was developed as a team effort by Jeffrey Liederman, big-game angler and proprietor of Capt. Harry's Fishing Supply, in Miami; Patrick Brown, a student work-

The SeaQualizer has proven instrumental in releasing a wide variety of bottom fish, especially red snapper.

ing on his master's degree in marine affairs and policy at the University of Miami; and Ryan Brown, a Florida International University graduate with a degree in civil engineering.

The trio felt the regulatory environment was ripe for an easier, quicker, safer and more effective way to release fish compared to venting. In addition to delivering a higher survival rate among released bottomfish, the men hope to show the governmental agencies that regulate recreational fishing that extreme rules and closures are not necessary to protect particular species. For example, consider zones entirely closed to fishing to protect a single species. Provided this device ensures the safe release of protected species

caught incidentally, it's feasible that such a zone could remain open to fishing for other species. This tool could have a major impact on recreational angling regulations.

How It Works

The SeaQualizer works by recompressing fish. That is, it takes a fish back down through the water column, where the increasing pressure on the swim bladder compresses the internal gasses so the fish can swim about as it did prior to being captured. It should be noted that recompression is already used in many regions to successfully release bottomfish, with techniques that involve sending fish down in weighted baskets or to the bottom on

weights. Yet the SeaQualizer offers additional advantages: ease of operation and the precision of freeing a fish at one of three preset depths. It is not necessary to lower a fish clear to the bottom before it is released.

The SeaQualizer has a locking grip that fastens to a fish's jaw much like a scale or release device. It also contains an internal pressure chamber and a three-setting adjustment knob at its opposite end. This adjustment controls the pressure at which the jaws open to release the fish. It can be set to open at 50, 100 or 150 feet. To send the SeaQualizer, a 5-pound weight and a fish into the depths, I used a heavy conventional rod paired with a conventional low-speed reel filled with heavy line, as suggested. My Penn Senator 114H2 has a 2.9:1 gear ratio, which made it easy to crank up the heavy lead after the release. The 100-pound-test braid coming off the rod tip was tied to a three-way swivel, and each of the two remaining eyes of the swivel had a small monofilament loop affixed. The 5-pound weight was tied to a short length of heavy monofilament with a longline clip at the opposite end, which clipped the weight to the mono ring on the lower ring eye of the swivel. The SeaQualizer also has a longline clip for securing it to the other mono ring on the swivel eye.

Proof at 100 Feet

Off Sarasota, we were jigging along the bottom in 230 feet of water. It was closed season on red snapper, so releases were in order for the ones we caught. Anxious to try out the SeaQualizer, I kept the release rod in a gunwale holder and rested the 5-pound weight in another rod holder. When we caught a red snapper, we affixed the SeaQualizer's locking grip to the lower jaw of the snapper, eased over the sash weight and fish, and then slowly backed off on the star drag. We watched as the weight and fish penetrated the clear blue Gulf water.

When we fought snapper to the surface, they were bloated and their scales appeared about to pop off. A couple even had their bladders protruding from their mouths. Yet, amazingly, once the fish were down between 30 and 50 feet and the recompression began, they became active. A bit deeper, right about where the

The SeaQualizer components. This red snapper is about to be "Seaqualized", safely and effectively.

The "release" outfit, SeaQualizer, and lead stick.

release clip opened, the fish were fighting to free themselves. On more than one occasion, we saw the locking grip open and the fish swim toward the bottom. It was amazing to watch.

Prior to this trip, I reviewed an underwater video showing Liederman and crew fishing in 330 feet of water off Miami, catching snowy grouper, tilefish, and vermilion and yellow-eye snappers. I watched two separate releases in which a bloated snowy grouper was attached to the SeaQualizer and lowered to the 100-foot mark, where the clip was programmed to open. Initially and down through the first 30 feet or so, the groupers simply twirled about, still suffering from barotrauma. But as they spiraled downward, the fish appeared to get thinner from the recompression, and friskier. Toward the end, they were fighting to

get off the grip. And when the grip opened, they swam off toward bottom, appearing none the worse for wear. My findings mirrored this video.

Liederman confirms that this process is much easier for both angler and fish than venting. Plus it's not necessary to lower the fish to the bottom. Based on the depth you're fishing, recompression can be successful at 50 feet, 100 feet or 150 feet. If you're bottomfishing in 100 feet of water, the shallow setting should suffice. Between 100 and 200 feet, the midrange setting should work, and beyond 200 feet, the deep setting. And how do you know exactly how deep the device (and fish) really is? Simply mark the line on the release rod at 50-foot intervals.

I honestly feel this tool will be on many a boat that partakes in bottomfishing, regardless of region. It's so

good that I wouldn't be surprised if it becomes mandatory for bottomfishing in certain waters, just like the venting tool is today. It's that cutting-edge. ✳

Availability

Liederman says the SeaQualizer will be available through retailers in January 2012. By the time you read this, though, the device will be in full production. The price has yet to be determined, but Liederman says it will be attractive and within most budgets.

For more information on the SeaQualizer and to order one when it becomes available, call 305-494-3408 or e-mail seaqualizer@gmail.com.

A Place for Everything: Having a neatly arranged tackle box makes fishing more efficient. Organization pays dividends in the form of more fish.

Chapter 4
Organize Your Tackle
Organized fishing gear is a trait of the successful angler

A quick change enabled Carl Grassi and me to convert a trio of amberjack into catches (and releases). We were drifting and fishing jigs and bucktails for groupers on the Abaco, Bahamas, reefs. At around 130 feet, a hump appeared on the fish finder, along with a few marks that weren't groupers or yellowtails. We took note and repositioned ourselves for another drift.

I went into my tackle bag, opened a plastic compartment, selected a 5-ounce Williamson Benthos jig and replaced the lead-head jig and ballyhoo combo in less than a minute. Grassi repositioned the boat, and we dropped down to enjoy a flurry with those amberjacks. My ability to quickly put my lure of choice into service was the result of having organized tackle boxes. When a situation requires tackle modification, losing time locating that right lure, hook, sinker or swivel has a steep price: a missed opportunity. Anglers need to react to a tackle change as rapidly as an Indy 500 pit crew to servicing a race car. And in the fishing world, efficiency lies in how well those tackle trays are organized.

Divide and Conquer

To promote efficiency, I divide my tackle bags and trays according to the type of fishing I plan to do. I have a few offshore bags, a few reef bags and a few inshore bags. Within each tackle bag are plastic tackle trays, with items organized by size, action and even intended species. Take my jigging trays, for example. I have separate trays devoted to bucktails, conventional deep jigs and flutter-style jigs. When Grassi and I got into those amberjacks, I simply opened my reef bag, took out the tray with the larger flutter-style irons and selected my jig. Organizing the jigs, I isolated the casting sizes of both bucktails and flutter-style jigs into separate boxes. Should Spanish or Cero mackerel pop up on

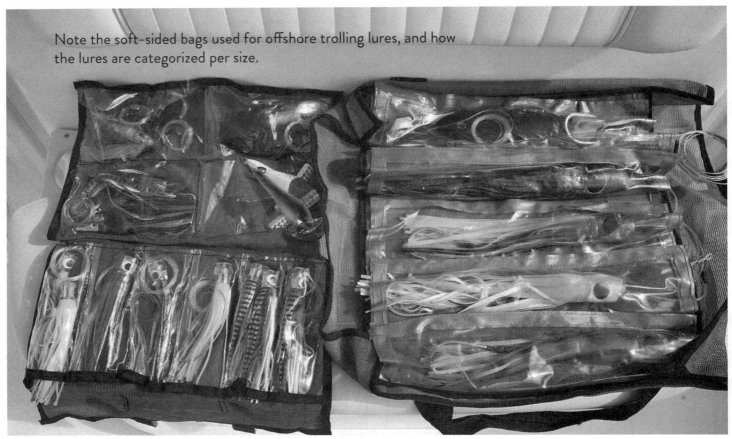

Note the soft-sided bags used for offshore trolling lures, and how the lures are categorized per size.

the reefs, or blackfin tuna and school dolphin offshore, I could easily find bucktails from 1/16 through 3 ounces in all colors or flutter-style jigs from 11/16 through 2¼ ounces. Again, no rummaging through an assortment of sizes and styles to find the right one. These bags store neatly in my tackle garage. And this enables me to mix and match certain trays for the fishing I plan on doing. For example, if we want to chum up tuna with live baits and catch them on topwater lures, I'll make sure to pack my topwater and sinking-lure trays in my offshore bag and leave the trays with offshore-trolling and bait-rigging gear behind. The ability to assemble specific boxes for any specialty fishing is really a neat deal.

Inshore, In-line

Categorizing carries to my inshore lures. For example, I maintain individual trays for topwater, sinking and swimming baits, and also soft baits. Should I desire a topwater lure to pitch

at seatrout, snook or tarpon, I retrieve my topwater tray, which contains a few sizes and colors of Rapala Skitter Walks and Skitter Pops and similar-style lures. My sinking-lure trays contain weighted hard baits, like X-Rap SubWalks, Glidin' Raps and Rattlin' Rapalas, whereas the swimming tray contains lipped shallow- and deep-diving lures. The soft-plastics trays reveal various sizes and hues of shrimp, crabs and minnow-style bodies. Again, the goal is quick and easy access to the right lures for any situation.

Organization is the same with small terminal items, such as swivels, which are categorized by barrel swivels, three-way swivels and trolling snap swivels in various sizes and strengths. There are also trays specifically for kite-fishing terminal items, such as rubber bands, floats, ceramic rings, release clips, rubber-core sinkers and balloons. The offshore-rigging tray has needles, floss, assorted sleeves, thimbles, crimpers and small sinkers.

Where's the Hook?

Aboard my boat, the hook trays get the most use. Imagine the range of hook variations needed to cover live- and dead-baiting, from seatrout to swordfish. For rigging trolling baits such as ballyhoo, mullet, mackerel and squid, I have trays with nothing but O'Shaughnessy-style hooks in various strengths and sizes, along with several specialty trolling-style hooks.

The live-bait-style hooks, in-line circle hooks in various strengths from 1/0 through 16/0, are categorized in circle-hook trays. What's more, the smaller and lighter-wire hooks are confined to one tray, which I use for seatrout on up to sailfish, whereas the heavier-wire and larger circle hooks are in a separate tray, for big grouper on up to yellowfin tuna and sharks. There are also individual trays for J hooks.

When we anchor on the reefs and chum, I remove the trays with the small circle hooks (for yellowtail, muttons, mackerel and kingfish) and also the small bucktails and flutter-style jigs, since this is what we use for the mackerel, amberjacks and horse-eye jacks. I keep the trays either on or near the console, where we all can work out of them. Before we leave, we return the trays to their respective tackle bags.

The Offshore Fellas

Offshore trolling lures, while not kept in plastic tackle trays, are organized by size and species sought. They are assigned to lure bags. For example, if we desire to mix some lures into our spread for dolphin, I'll fetch a lure bag containing small flat-, blunt- and concave-head lures rigged on leaders ranging from 50- to 130-pound-test. Conversely, if we see blackfins or yellowfins, there's another soft-lure bag with small bullet- and jet-head-style lures rigged on 30- to 80-pound-test fluorocarbon. And of course, we have individual bags with larger marlin lures and wahoo lures.

Container Carl

My friend Carl Grassi is not only a good angler but also meticulous when it comes to storing his tackle. In fact, I recently learned something from him. Rather than keep his accessories, such as knives, leaders and boat parts, on his vessel, he puts them in plastic carry boxes. This way, if he needs fillet knives back at the dock, there's no rummaging through his boat to find them. He merely goes into his console and retrieves his knife box, where you'll find several knives,

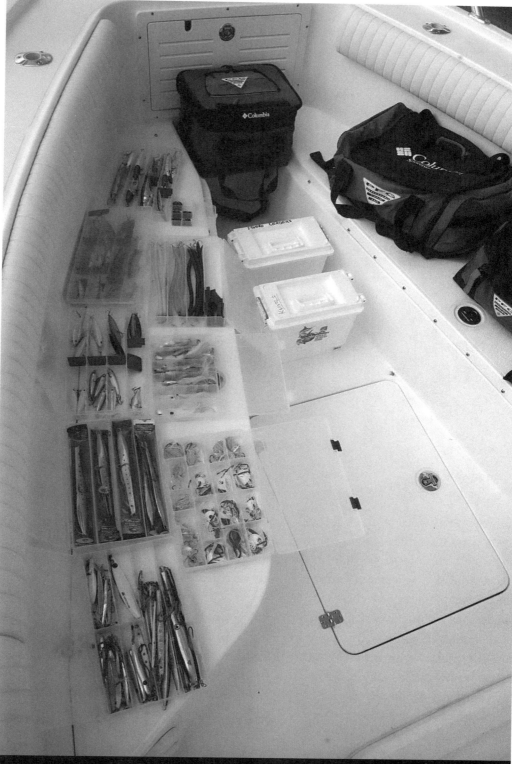

Here's a peek at how some of the tackle aboard the MARC VI is organized. Note the specific lures and jigs in their own trays, the soft bags that contain these trays, and the containers designated for spools of leader, and also knives. Everything is simple and quick to get to.

a sharpening stone and even freezer bags for his fillets. What's neat is that he can wash, dry and oil down these

knives before they're packed away, keeping them clean and rust-free.
I've gone this route with my

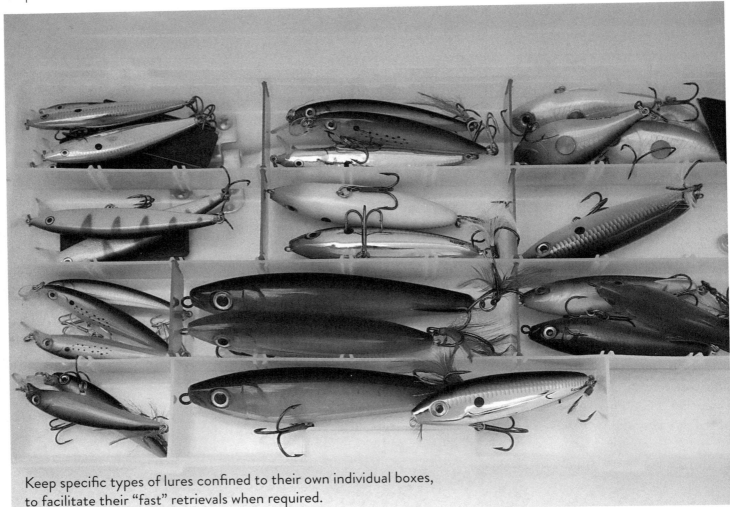

Keep specific types of lures confined to their own individual boxes, to facilitate their "fast" retrievals when required.

knives, spools of leader material and spare parts (fuel filters and hoses for those Bahamas crossings). It takes just a tad longer to add and remove these containers from the boat, but the advantages include easy access (on the boat and in your garage), less exposure to a saltwater environment and the elements, and a smaller chance of theft if kept permanently on board.

If you're already taking care of your tackle in this fashion, go to the head of the class; you're able to concentrate more on catching fish when you're on the water. If your tackle organization program is running a little behind, remember this article during the next rainy weekend; it will give you plenty to do and something even to curse over if your tackle is really disorganized. But once you've arranged everything, there will be a big difference in your efficiency the next time you set forth. And efficiency and preparedness are two classic traits of successful anglers worldwide.

Keep 'em Clean

There are few things I despise more than seeing a used saltwater hook, lure or jig returned to its tray without a freshwater rinse. If you return something without rinsing it, expect rust and corrosion to spread throughout that tray like wildfire, ruining your investment.

On my boat, all used lures, hooks, jigs and such are kept in a bucket or sink until it's time to wash down the boat. During this process, they'll get a freshwater rinsing, a soaping and another freshwater rinsing. I hang the gear on a shelf in my garage for several days, and then — and only then — put them back into their respective tackle trays.

Keep 'em Ready to Go

In addition to keeping your terminal tackle organized and readily accessible, it's smart practice to rig a few extra rods with the lures, jigs and hooks that might come into play during your fishing day. This way, should any opportunities arise beyond your chosen method of fishing that day, you'll be covered. For example, when trolling offshore, we'll have several spinners rigged with bucktails and plain hooks. Should we troll up a school of dolphin, we're set to take advantage of them. Or if we see a large solitary fish, we have the option of pitch-baiting a dead or live bait. There's also a small conventional outfit rigged with a flutter-style jig, for dropping deep under boards, debris, large weed patches and school dolphin, where wahoo often lurk. ✳

Night lights, both portable and in-hull, are essential to stirring up action at dark, as is obvious by this Mako shark.

Chapter 5

The Shine of Fishing Lights
Light 'em up for more hook ups!

Fishing lights have long been advantageous, and often essential, for scoring in both fresh and salt waters. The ever-changing technology in the electronics/lighting field has resulted in a new generation of fish-attracting, marine game fish lights, in both portable and in-hull versions.

Quality fishing lights do four distinct things: draw, illuminate, entertain, and produce. With the former, the brightness permeating through dark waters acts as a "visual chum". That is, it attracts the food chain, from baitfish on up to predators lured in by both the forage species and brightness. Next, a quality light or lighting system will illuminate a large area – if not the entire space - around a boat. In turn, this provides a "focal point" for anglers to not only fish or place baits along

its shadow line (where the brightness fades to darkness – prime ambush points for game fish), but also to see and quickly react to any large fish entering that visual zone. It entertains because just about everything from baitfish to squid to juvenile game fish often swim through the illuminated area. So, while waiting on the target fish, impatient anglers can keep busy jigging squid or baitfish or dip-netting tiny pelagics for a quick study. And, of course, fishing lights help put more fish in the boat, compared to non-illuminated vessels. Credit that to their drawing bait around a boat - enabling those baits to be caught and deployed - and also large pelagics. Naturally, a good angler helps tremendously with the latter!

Fishing lights once again proved their worth during a recent "over-

nighter" in the Wilmington Canyon off Avalon, New Jersey, where Captain Joe Trainor, Trey Rhyne and I scored a couple of Mako sharks. In both instances, the Mako was lurking beyond the shadow line from the green, portable Hydro Glow light, and "teased" into eating a bait. The light lured in the squid, which we jigged for live bait, and also those sharks. And as mentioned earlier, the illuminated swath of water made it easy to see and react to the sharks, which made baiting them easier. In addition to the Makos, several blue sharks kept everyone on their toes beyond the midnight hour.

For "in-hull" fishing lights, LED technology now provides for an ultra strong product that can withstand the pounding and abuse of boats running in rough seas, while drawing little amperage. Also, unlike Halogen and

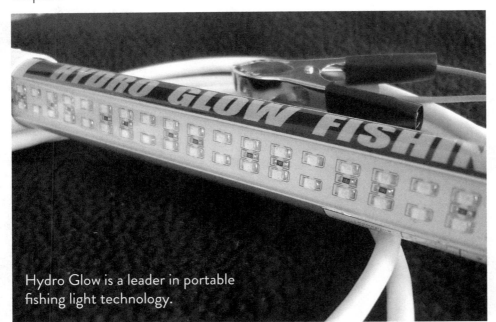

Hydro Glow is a leader in portable fishing light technology.

name 13 years ago with a four-foot long, fluorescent green tube light, complete with terminals that attach to a battery - which they still offer today. According to company president and angler Darrell Keith, his product was born out of necessity for a light that would not only stay underwater (not float), but also be efficient enough to operate all night without draining its battery. His Hydro Glows do just that and are precision-balanced to where they'll submerge fully upright, and – in essence – broadcast 360-degrees of lighting around a boat. Constructed for the rigors of a saltwater environment, their bulbs have a 20,000 hour life expectancy. These lights continue to be used widely for not only swordfish, tuna and sharks, but also inshore fishing for fluke, flounder, redfish, seatrout, snook and tarpon – as well as baitfish. They retail for around $ 200.00. Hydro Glow also makes lights for fresh water pan-fishing, and underwater dock lights.

Xenon/HID, LED lights do not throw off excessive heat and will not be damaged or ruined if accidentally left on when the boat is removed from the water. Also surface mount "in-hull" lights are becoming more in vogue, compared to thru-hull units, where drilling a large hole in the vessel below the water line, and installing related fittings are required. By comparison, most surface mount lights require just a single wire to be run through the hull, and for them to be affixed to the hull with screws.

Listed below are just three examples of cutting-edge fishing lights. These three companies – one marketing a highly-popular portable unit and two marketing "in hull" systems – are utilizing LED technology to achieve a brighter and greater "throw" of light with minimum battery drain. Here's a peek at what they have to offer.

HYDRO GLOW (www.hydroglow.com - 877-895-4569) – Long considered the leader in portable saltwater fishing lights, Hydro Glow made their

In the LED category, Hydro Glow has one-foot long, and two-foot long models, with 162 LEDs and 324 LEDs, respectively. These lightweight lights

COLOR VERSUS COLOR, PORTABLE VERSUS IN-HULL

As far as the most productive fishing light color, in general, that still remains a matter of opinion, although blue has become very popular as of late. Captain Bouncer Smith has spent a ton of nights swordfishing and bait fishing in the waters off South Florida, and, as always, has his opinions. "We've been fishing the green Hydro Glow light for a long, long time and catching a lot of fish with it," says Bouncer. "I later changed to a blue one, because fish can see the color blue from a farther distance than the green. Well, we caught a lot of fish with the blue light, but I can't say it was drastically different over what we caught using the green light. But what I do notice, is that the green light draws things closer to it, and with the blue light we rarely see things close to the boat – they seem to stay farther back. So green is better for bringing fish closer to the boat, in my opinion."

As far as portable fish lights versus in-hull lights, that's largely an issue of what you're fishing for and where, how often you fish in darkness, how cool you want your boat to look, and, of course, budget. Bouncer reports that with his Hydro Glow, he sees all the way around his boat, from transom to bow. He is currently using blue lights affixed to the underside of his engine bracket and aimed straight down. "These transom lights are more limited in the area they service, and don't illuminate the water like the Hydro Glow does" says Bouncer.

Based on Bouncer's findings, it stands to reason that gaining a strong broadcasting from in-hull lights boils down to the number of lights you can afford to install in the boat, and the positioning of these lights. Some of the best arranged in-hull fish lights shoot not only directly out from the transom, but are also mounted underneath the hull so they'll also shoot downward. However, that being said, some ultra-bright LED hull lights deliver strong coverage of both distance and depth shooting directly out from the back of the transom, by simply going with multiple units.

The author's center console, pictured here on its trailer, utilizes four Shadow-Caster surface mount lights, in Bimini Blue. The lights' diminutive size and stylish look, make them appear as if they're from the boat manufacturer itself. They're constructed with 316 stainless steel and polycarbonate housings. All that's necessary to mount them is a small hole for its submersible grade cable, and two screws.

have an 80,000 hour life expectancy. Like their predecessors, they are submergible and have weathered pressure changes down to 50-feet. They're available in blue or green, and sell for around $ 95.00 (one-foot model) and $ 169.99 (two-foot model).

Also due out this December is a four-foot LED model designed exclusively for swordfish and tuna. It will contain over 600 LED lights, and – according to Darrell Keith – will be the brightest and most durable portable light on the market. The unit is one-inch in diameter, with strips of LED lights mounted on three sides of the light for a full, 360-degree "throw". It's touted as drawing only 2- amps, and will come in green or blue/violet.

Expect it to sell for around $ 239.00.

LUMISHORE (www.lumishore. com) – A leading provider of innovative, bright, high-quality LED marine light for yachts, pleasure and fishing vessels, Lumishore now offers a line of surface mount fishing lights in white, blue and green. Models SMX 20 (830 Lumens), 50 (1210 Lumens) and 100 (2310 Lumens) have power comparable to that of a 50, 75, and 150 watt Xenon light, respectively, and a 50,000 hour life-expectancy. At 12 volts, they'll draw 1A, 1.5A, and 3A, respectively, whereas at 24 volts they'll draw 0.5A, 0.75A, and 1.5A.

Coming this November will be model SM150-CCP (Color Change Plus).

TO STROBE OR NOT TO STROBE?
"Strobing", incidentally is becoming more popular with fishing lights, as that "pulsing" and "flashing" has proven advantageous in attracting fish. Could it be the illusion is perceived as the reflection of baitfish, or, perhaps, is it simply the constant flashing that catches the attention of fish?

Strobing can involve a quick, repetitive cycle, which could be perceived by game fish as frantic baitfish, or a more spaced out cycle, which predator fish could perceive as calm, schooling fish unaware of its presence. Then, add in the various colors to "strobe" with, and you get an idea just how fine-tuned an illusion one can create.

Expect to see this feature become even more commonplace in the near future.

This surface mount model (2 lights and a controller), which draws 5A at 12-volts and 2.5A at 24-volts and has a power equivalent to a 150-watt Xenon light,

The author's center console, pictured here at rest in the Bahamas, sports four Shadow-Caster model SCM-10V2 surface mount lights in Bimini Blue.

comes with a full color spectrum control – blue, white, cyan, green, magenta and red. It will feature three strobe speeds (as little as 30-seconds and as long as a couple of minutes) for any chosen color, and three selectable output intensities in preset colors.

"The system is purchased as a set of two lights and a controller", says Lumishore's Keith Wansley. The controller allows you to scroll through six standard colors, as well as activate the strobing. So, if you wish, you can illuminate the water in six rotating colors, or the ones of your choosing. Should more lights be desired, the original controller can handle up to 14 lights. We anticipate the new SM150-CCP to retail for around $ 3,000.00 (two lights and a controller).

SHADOW-CASTER MARINE
LEDs (www.shadow-caster.com -727-474-2877) – One of the hot-

test surface mount fishing lights on the market is Shadow-Caster. These high-intensity LED underwater lights are manufactured with 316 stainless steel and polycarbonate housings and have a life expectancy of 40,000 hours. The three models include SCM-4 (17 Watt), SCM-6 (24 Watt) and SCM-10V2 (42 Watt), which are also available with wireless controller with key fob to control dimming and strobing of the lights. The lights are each priced at around $ 479.00, $ 549.00 and $ 679.00, respectively.

What I found on equal par to the lights performance is their relatively diminutive size, which provides a lot of latitude on where to mount them. For example, I have four pairs of model SCM-10V2 neatly arranged on the transom of my Mako 284 – shooting outward, for a bright and powerful throw. This model measures 10-inches in width, 2.25-inches in height, and 1/2-inch in thickness. Their smallest model (SCM-4), incidentally, measures 5.8-inches wide, 2.375-inches in height and 1/2-inch thick. Given their sharp-looking 316 stainless steel frames, they appear more like a standard feature of the boat – right from the factory - rather than an "add on" aftermarket option. And with most boats sporting aluminum towers, rails or trim, they blend right in.

These lights were developed by Brian Rogers – an electrical and optical engineer, and Jeff Pound - a military electronics design engineer, hence their "toughness" in a saltwater environment - even when coupled with boats that are trailered.

The Shadow-Casters come in Great White, Aqua Green, Bimini Blue, Ultra Blue, and Cool Red (I've Bimini Blue). Current draw is 1.4A at 12 volts, and the lights generate over 2,000 Lumens. To mount, they require just

a small hole for its submersible grade cable, and two screws. The units have internal thermal throttling circuitry, which keeps them from getting too hot should they be left on when the boat is out of the water. Additionally, they include robust internal transient surge protection, which protects the microprocessor controlled switching power supply from dirty marine electrical systems.

Brand new this November will be their Color Caster model (a 10V2 size unit), which will include 10 LEDs with each LED capable of changing to one of four colors. The light will be controlled by one switch, quickly cycling power to rotate the color. One mode will fade the lights through all four colors, whereas another mode will fade between just the blue and white lights (their two most popular colors). Best yet, these new lights will fit in the same footprint as their current ones, for easy upgrades. Pricing has yet to be set for this light. ✻

BOUNCER'S THREE MOST IMPORTANT TIPS WHEN USING FISHING LIGHTS

1.) When fishing a portable light in waters up to 40- or 50-feet deep, attach a float (Styrofoam, etc.) to the light to keep it near the surface and set it a few feet away from the boat. Doing so will keep the light from rocking with the boat, which could diminish its uniform throw of light.

2.) Fish the edges of the light where it reaches toward the bottom, and also the perimeters of the lighted area.

3.) Attach one or two Strip Teaser strands fairly close to a portable fishing light (on power cord), which will mimic baitfish flashing near the light. This will, in turn, attract more baitfish and ultimately game fish.

The Knocker Rig is deadly effective on a wide variety of bottom fish, including this grouper, and can also "probe" into crevices with minimal snags.

Chapter 6
The Poveromo Knocker-Rig
Try this proven rig when fishing for stubborn grouper and snapper on the reefs

The yellowtail bite was fast and furious, as expected along this Bimini, Bahamas reef. Almost as quick as we'd drift a bait back, we'd pluck a plump yellowtail from the sea. Balls of the golden fish materialized within the water, the more aggressive 'tails moving to within a few feet of our chum bag. Then, suddenly, they disappeared, as if sucked back into their lairs by some huge vacuum. Predator fish had moved in.

A few large reefs sharks convened deep behind our boat, looking for a snapper struggling on a hook, an easy meal, and the yellowtails wanted no part

of that game. Our small silverside-tipped jigs and pieces of bait drifting with the chum had just become obsolete. To continue catching 'tails, we'd have to bait them on the bottom, and on tackle just heavy enough to crank them up through the water column ahead of the sharks. It was time to change up.

I grabbed two of the larger spinning outfits, both of which were spooled with 30-pound-test braid. I rerigged them with 15 feet of 20-pound-test fluorocarbon leader and a 5/0 in-line circle hook. Before securing the hook to the leader, I added a 2-ounce egg sinker, which rested on the eye of the hook. This is

what is known as a knocker rig.

We baited the hooks with pieces of bonito and ballyhoo and dropped the knocker rigs to the bottom. Nearly instantly the snappers consumed the baits, and we rapidly wound them up to the boat, with sharks in hot pursuit. When the score was tallied, we'd won far more of these drag races than the sharks had. But the bottom line was that, once again, the knocker rig paid dividends for us!

Defying Bad Structure for Decades

BottomFishing 101 tells us that using

This large mutton snapper, caught by a smiling Andrea Pallavicini, fell for a live pinfish on a knocker rig.

This monster Florida snook was caught on a live pilchard pinned to a knocker rig, and fished along an inlet bottom.

the lightest weight possible to hold a bait on or near bottom while keeping that weight away from the hook is paramount in catching a variety of benthic species. This could range from a hook and sinker separated by just 2 or 3 feet of leader and a swivel for striped bass and snook in inlets or around bridges to a sinker above a 15- to 30-foot-long leader intended to fool mutton snapper. The objective here is to lessen the resistance a fish feels when it picks up, mouths or nibbles at a bait and encourage it to devour that bait and not drop it. This is accomplished through the extra latitude and even slack provided by a long leader coming off of a sinker. The fish takes the bait and feels nothing unnatural until the hook is set and it's too late.

However, logic does have its limits. And in this case, high-profile

and rugged structure - such as ragged reefs, rock piles, wrecks and even kelp gardens - becomes the game-changer. When you're looking to drop a bait into such dangerous terrain, the knocker rig becomes a worthy ally.

Bouncer and the Knocker

Capt. Bouncer Smith has long been regarded as the premier inlet, reef and offshore skipper in Florida's Miami-Dade County. Many believe he has no peer when it comes to catching a wide variety of game fish the likes of snook, tarpon, grouper, snapper, sailfish, kingfish, cobia, dolphin, swordfish and numerous other fish swimming in the local waters. And when it comes to bottomfishing along the reefs and wrecks off southern Florida and Bimini, he gives the knocker rig its share of play.

"The concept of the knocker rig is sort of like dropping into a forest of snagging trees," says Smith. "The sinker and bait stay together as the rig enters into a heavy-growth reef, so it won't start off tangled. The sinker stays in place, and the fish can't tell the difference between the sinker and a rock. With a long leader rig - let's say 4 feet long - the sinker will land on bottom, while the leader may snag two or three rocks in the process."

Smith uses the knocker rig to catch just about all snappers and contends it can be used for all sorts of bottom- and near-bottom-dwelling fish that thrive in and around ragged structure. Furthermore, the rig works in conjunction with live or dead baits.

Uneven Weight Distribution

Contrary to the philosophy of us-

A circle-hook knocker rig is a "knock out" on bottom fish, like this grouper.

ing the lightest weight possible to reach and hold bottom, lighter is not necessarily better with the knocker rig. Smith says the weight should be plenty heavy, enough to remain in solid contact with the bottom. And as simple as this rig appears, there are indeed subtleties involved in getting the most out of it. "You want to feel the sinker at all times," says Smith. "Once it's on bottom, you will reel up just enough to where you feel the weight. You will then actively hold the rod and make certain to feel that sinker at all times. That means you'll lower the rod when the boat lifts up on a wave, to keep the sinker on bottom, and lift the rod when the boat dips down, to maintain the feel of the sinker on bottom. To make sure the rig is where it's supposed to be and to sense the slightest activity from any fish playing with the bait, you have to keep enough

slack out of the line so you can feel the sinker and keep it in place on the bottom.

"It's also critical to make sure when tying the line to the hook that the knot doesn't jam in the sinker, as could happen if the sinker has a large enough hole. If this occurs, it will prevent a fish from running line through the sinker and perhaps enable it to feel the weight and drop the bait. To prevent this, put a plastic bead on the line before tying on the hook. The plastic bead will rest between the sinker and hook eye and prevent jamming."

Where Lighter Is Better

One case in which going with a lighter sinker takes precedence is when you're baiting fish that are suspending within or adjacent to high-profile debris or structure, such as snapper around rigs and even Pacific yellowtail and kelp bass within kelp gardens. Here a lighter sinker enables the bait to settle a bit slower through the water column and stay where these fish are suspending. In the case of kelp gardens and rig stanchions, a knocker rig will keep the bait and hook together throughout the descent, while a longer leader has the potential to wrap around both sides of the kelp or stanchions.

As mentioned earlier, the knocker rig kept us into the yellowtail snapper action when the predator fish drove them down. Even when the 'tails are up and close to the boat, we often pitch a knocker rig well back into

the slick, where it falls to the bottom behind most of the activity. And quite often, we pick off our largest 'tails that way. Just recently we spent a day on a different Bimini reef, dropping live pilchards on knocker rigs; we scored amberjack to 40 pounds, horse-eye jacks to 15 pounds and, of course, yellowtail snapper. The setup is excellent on mangrove snapper on the reefs and rock piles, and we've scored cobia and goliath grouper on the knocker rigs when fishing over wrecks.

In-line, non-stainless-steel circle hooks make effective knocker rigs, and they're required by law when bottom-fishing in the Gulf of Mexico. I prefer using an overhand loop knot to join my circle hook to the leader, believing that the loop gives a live bait pinned to the knocker-rig hook more freedom to swim. And when the bite's slow, I believe that extra bit of freedom prompts more strikes. What's more, a properly lodged circle hook will remain intact, while a J-style hook becomes more susceptible to being thrown with that sinker riding so close.

Newcomers to the knocker rig often wonder why a fish wouldn't notice a lead sitting right on top of the hook and shy away from the rig. My answer to that question is that game fish strike deep jigs and even jigs tipped with bait - so why would the knocker rig look much different, save for the lack of a fancy coat of paint?

The next time you find yourself wanting to cull bottomfish from tough terrain, don't outthink yourself by dropping down fancy leaders and rigs, which just might tangle or snag. Give the knocker rig some soak time. It's certainly not much appearance-wise, but it has been catching bottomfish for decades, making many a marginal angler look like a rock star back at the dock. ✳

There's no doubting the fish-raising abilities of the cedar plug. But, could they be fine-tuned to be even more potent?

Chapter 7
The Cedar Plug Lives On
Some classic lures just won't go away - for good reason...

I have a love-hate relationship with cedar plugs. I'm fond of the antiquated lures' ability to raise lots of fish, and I detest them because of the numerous fish that are lost to pulled hooks.

Recently I presented a Trolling Tactics panel for the SWS National Seminar Series at the Jersey Shore, in New Jersey, and expressed my views on cedar plugs to panel member Trey Rhyne, an ardent offshore-trolling authority and head of Over Under Sportfishing. Rhyne quickly replied: "Well, if you want to catch fish, put

the cedar plugs out there. If you don't, keep them in the boat. I'd much rather get the bites and risk losing a fish or two than not get a strike." Valid point indeed, Trey! But then things got interesting when we got into why fish seem to pull free from them and how to possibly modify them to "stick" better. More on all this later.

Not the Pick of the Litter
When it comes to offshore-trolling lures, the cedar plug is arguably the plain Jane of the lot. It lacks the sleek design and snazzy paint schemes of

most modern lures, many of which resemble Indy 500 race cars. In fact, the cedar plug is more akin to a '57 Chevy. But what this ancient lure lacks in modern luster, it makes up for in fresh meat. These lures have been used worldwide for decades, and the number of fish they've accounted for is mind-boggling.

In their basic form, cedar plugs are relatively short and plump pencil-like lures which dart frantically when trolled, not unlike walk-the-dog-style surface plugs. Their wild action and diminutive size make them attractive

Cedar plugs are tuna magnets, as evidenced by these Jersey canyon yellowfins.

and easy-to-consume targets. They can be trolled solo or in a daisy chain. And as simplistic as they appear, there is some rhyme and reason to how and where to fish them. Enter Capt. Joe Trainor.

A Cedar Kind of Guy

Trainor is a noted big-game captain who plies the waters of the Bahamas and the Northeast for Over Under Sportfishing. I've fished with him on several occasions and scarcely recall him not dropping a cedar plug into the spread. "We fish them nearly every day in the Bahamas," says Trainor. "I fish them from the shotgun position, some 75 to 100 yards back, and as a daisy chain. I'll have three cedar plugs rigged on 130-pound-test monofilament leader, and each is staggered 18 inches apart. The first two cedar plugs are blue-and-white, and the last one,

a natural wood color, is rigged with a 10/0 long-shank needle-eye hook. We catch yellowfins on the cedar daisy chain - and wahoo, dolphin and even the occasional blue marlin.

"When trolled around 6 knots, the first two plugs track right along while the last one darts more erratically; it looks like a confused and injured bait," he says. "That's precisely the action that gets the strikes." Furthermore, Trainor secures a large barrel swivel behind all but the rear plug (which has the hook). These barrel swivels act as stops to keep the plugs 18 inches apart. Another advantage of the swivels is that if the rear plug gets bitten off by a wahoo or shark, another cedar plug on an 18-inch lead can quickly be secured to the swivel, and the rig goes right back into the game. In the Bahamas, Trainor trolls just one cedar-plug daisy chain in a spread of seven to eight baits.

The Jersey Connection

Off the Jersey coast, Trainor fishes single cedar plugs. Often he'll use a pair that rides between 50 and 75 yards back off a flat line secured to a transom clip and short outrigger clip. Colors include red- and-white, blue-and-white, and natural. "This seems to be a good position for the yellowfins, and a productive trolling speed for them is around 6 to 6½ knots," says Trainor. As in the Bahamas, each plug is rigged with 15 feet of 130-pound-test monofilament leader and a 10/0 needle-eye hook. "These join a spread of seven to eight baits and two spreader bars," Trainor says.

"Now, for school bluefins, fish averaging between 25 and 60 pounds, we fish two cedar plugs right in the prop wash, like from 15 to 40 feet back, from flat lines and transom clips," he continues. "I'll troll fewer baits for the

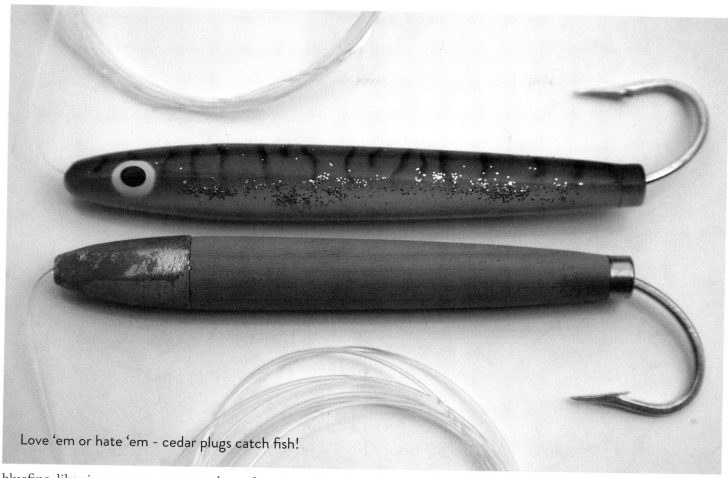

Love 'em or hate 'em - cedar plugs catch fish!

bluefins, like six or seven, one spreader bar and then the two single cedar plugs. Our best bluefin trolling speed is between 5 and 5½ knots."

Wind-On Joe

Trainor is a proponent of wind-on leaders, which eliminate the wiring of a cedar plug-hooked tuna. When someone takes the leader, the dynamics of the fight can be altered. And when that occurs, the lure may pull free. Trainor's preferred cedar-plug trolling setup is a Penn 50 International filled with 80-pound-test monofilament. A 15-foot 130-pound-test monofilament leader is joined to the fishing line with a 130-pound-test offshore wind-on swivel (which passes right through the guides). "I see guys pulling cedar plugs rigged to 6- and 8-foot leaders and large snap swivels," says Trainor. "I believe a large snap swivel placed so

close to a cedar plug takes away from its action. Plus, the commotion from that swivel can spook fish and keep them from striking."

Color Me a Fish

An old-timer once told a friend that he was appalled at the wide variety of colors modern cedar plugs come in. His reasoning was that the original cedar-plug material enabled the lures to be soaked in menhaden or other fish oils (below); the cedar wood absorbed the oils and held the scent, lending yet another element to the lure. This individual claimed the newer hard-plastic ones - and even the painted wooden models - don't absorb oils and scents and, therefore, aren't as good as the old ones.

Yet color has indeed become a factor. Trainor favors red-and-white cedar plugs on sunny days but is quick to

point out that blue-and-white remains a potent all-weather color combination, perhaps resembling flying fish. Other top captains troll cedar plugs in assorted colors and switch up if the fish are showing a preference for a specific hue.

Hold On, Gaff's a Coming

As mentioned earlier, my beef with cedar plugs has been over their dropping fish. Apparently this can be traced to the hook shank riding well inside the rear of the plug, with only the gap and point of the hook exposed. When a fish chomps on the plug, it's feasible the cedar plug could prevent the fish's jaws from fully closing and the hook from planting deeply and solidly. It's also feasible that, during the fight and especially when the boat maintains forward momentum, the plug design generates a certain amount of leverage that could work on the hook and free it.

The author caught this plump yellowfin on a cedar plug.

Joe Trainor, Trey Rhyne and I have kicked around some cedar-plug rigging ideas to promote better hookups. The most obvious is to increase the size of the hook, where the larger gap/bite would likely penetrate deeper. My thinking is to add a few spacer beads and position the hook outside of the cedar plug, some 1 to 2 inches behind the body (above). This way, the hook would be free and clear of the plug and more prone to latch onto a fish. Also, it may have a tendency to snag, providing yet another opportunity to catch a short-striking fish.

And while we're on the subject of experimentation, I'm not so sure a circle hook rigged in this fashion wouldn't be the bomb for catching fish. Think about it. Once the plug slides across a fish's jaws and the circle hook sets, there is no way short of breaking the line that the fish will get off. It's not out of the question: At one time no one would have thought that circle hooks on diamond, flutter-style or traditional jigs would have worked so well, but they do.

Two things are for sure: Cedar plugs catch fish, and thousands of them will be in tow this coming season. And you can bet that guys like Rhyne, Trainor and me will be experimenting with ways to make them stick better. If we're successful, I can finally profess my unconditional love for this relic of a hell-raiser! *

Match lure size and color to that of the local forage and you'll come up a winner.

Chapter 8
Six Topwater Secrets
Tailor your topwater tactics for tough fish

Captain Gary Dubiel is a master at catching fish on light tackle and artificial lures. A professional guide based in Oriental, North Carolina (www. specfever.com), he excels at everything from sea trout to the trophy drum that enter Pamlico Sound each fall. One of his favorite tactics is catching fish on topwater plugs, and he has a wealth of knowledge in that arena.

Just this past November, I fished with Gary in the Neuse and Trent rivers right out of New Bern, North Carolina. Our goal was to catch river-run striped bass on topwater plugs. Normally, given the amount of stripers in this system, that is an easy feat. On this trip, we found a lot of fish,

but they were finicky; it was obvious we weren't going to set the world on fire without digging deep into the bag of topwater tricks we'd both acquired over the years.

Gary and I hit on a number of combinations that fooled the fish, and we went on to enjoy some fast light-tackle fishing. Most anglers understand the basics of choosing and fishing topwater plugs, like matching the size and color of a lure to that of the local forage, mimicking the action of the local baitfish (whether they're being ambushed or simply milling near the surface) and tweaking retrieves until the right one is found. But beyond these basics, the following

"deeper" techniques can tip the odds in your favor when fish are reluctant to take part in the topwater game. Keep these in mind the next time you need a play called in from the sidelines.

1. Can You Hear Me Knocking?
Some topwater plugs have internal rattles, which telegraph noise and vibration farther than plugs without sound chambers. Rattles are excellent for enticing fish up from the deep or in from the distance. The resulting clacking/clicking vibrations replicate the sounds a frantic injured baitfish makes as it kicks its way across the surface. Sometimes that noise is exactly what pushes a game fish to strike.

Successfully fishing top water lures often comes down to matching the size of the local baitfish along with colors and shades.

On our North Carolina outing, Dubiel and I used Rapala Skitter Walk topwater plugs with rattles.

Conversely, I have experienced times when the rattle plugs have actually kept fish at bay. When fish are leery and seem more sensitive to noise, a topwater plug without a rattle could prove the way to go; sometimes it takes a softer, quieter, more subtle retrieve to get strikes. Keep both versions handy, and give them equal soak time to find out which one the fish prefer.

2. Leader Out

Another effective yet often overlooked trick - particularly in clear water - is keeping your leader out of the water. Again, when fish are off their feed, going with a smaller diameter, lighter leader is a basic adaptation. However, it's even more effective if most of that leader rides out of the water.

In the Neuse and Trent rivers, we were getting quite a few followers and last second turn-aways. Granted, the water there is far from clear, but these followers had plenty of time to investigate our lures. And, initially, something was keeping them from striking.

I began making long casts and holding my rod tip high over my head while imparting short twitches to create a tight walk-the-dog action. By holding the rod high, I kept most of that 25-pound test leader out of the water. The strikes started coming, and I believe my tactic had a lot to do with it.

3. Hit the Throttles

When fish are reluctant to strike, try teasing the followers by increasing retrieval speed as soon as you see them behind the lure. When fish are striking with abandon, keep to your original retrieve; it is

when strikes are slow in coming that this trick shines.

Think about it. If you were a fish that had just charged up behind a lure, and that lure just kept twitching along with no appreciable difference in action, wouldn't you think something was amiss? In nature, that fleeing baitfish should sense a predator fish coming at it, and the realization that it is just seconds from doom should prompt it to panic. The ensuing change in speed and distress vibrations are what often prompts a game fish into striking, triggering its natural instincts to prey on this weak link - hungry or not.

On several occasions, we sped up our lures when fish appeared behind them to create the illusion of their trying to outrun the fish. Between that tease and keeping most of the leader out of the water, several followers were converted into releases.

Fine-tune the speed and retrieve of your top water lure until you find the combination fish like.

4. Do the Locomotion

A radical modification, which was not put into play during my trip with Dubiel, is creating the illusion of a pair or more of baitfish scurrying away from feeding fish. The simplest way to do this is to tie a topwater plug about 3 feet behind a popping cork. Cast the rig and then retrieve it by popping the cork and occasionally letting the rig rest for a couple of seconds. This creates the illusion of a smaller baitfish bird-dogging a larger injured bait. Most of the strikes should come on the smaller rear plug.

Another setup is to use the same style, size and color of plugs. To be sporting, and so it poses less risk of injury to angler and fish, remove the

An overhand loop knot is recommended for joining lure to leader.

Chugger-type lures are great for sending sounds and vibrations far throughout the water.

hooks on the lead lure. Tie the leader to the lure's eye. Then tie a 2- or 3-foot leader to the rear eye of the plug, and that leader to the lead eye of the rear plug. You can add a third plug by removing its hooks and adding it to the lineup. With both two and three lures, this rig can be worked in a number of ways, ranging from twitching and pausing under a slow retrieve to a slightly quicker, more radical retrieve with aggressive side-to-side action. While the lead plugs might draw strikes some of the time, it is usually the last plug in line that catches fish.

5. Hit the Brakes

One of Dubiel's favorite tricks is to pause his topwater plug. There are occasions, especially during feeding blitzes, when fish refuse to strike a rapidly moving plug. Perhaps the fish become programmed to consume the injured ones that can't swim off? Fish that aren't especially aggressive sometimes want an easier target, like a severely injured bait that is barely kicking.

I watched Dubiel convert many a fish by occasionally pausing his lure for a few seconds before picking up the retrieve and pausing the lure again for a few more seconds. This tactic worked well when he pitched a lure right into the blitz, where you would think any quickly fleeing lure would draw strikes.

6. Color Me Gone

As mentioned earlier, matching the hatch in terms of size and coloration is generally a smart move. Yet as much as I subscribe to this theory and stick to my guns, like I did in New Bern, North Carolina, sometimes it takes some experimentation to get the bites. I fished mainly a silver with black-back plug, to imitate finger mullet, and occasionally a menhaden-hued plug, since peanut bunker were also amassing. However, Dubiel selects colors that offer the most visibility in those tannin-stained waters. He favors chartreuse plugs or those with highlights of chartreuse - a color I've yet to see in

any natural baitfish - which he claims permeates these waters farther than other colors and makes the plugs more visible to fish. I can't argue with him since he scores on them.

When the natural-hued plugs aren't cutting it, pick a radical color, such as pure white, chartreuse, orange or even black, and give it a try. Perhaps you'll find one that is indeed more visible to fish. It might not appear natural colorwise, but the silhouette it presents might just be strong enough to stand out to a fish. Add in a little action, and the rest, as they say, might be history - for the fish, that is!

Fishing topwater plugs is an art. Sometimes the bite is on, and all that's necessary is to pitch out the lure. Yet tough times dictate some thinking, and that's when a lot of anglers give up on topwaters. For me, watching a fish explode on a topwater plug is one of the neatest sights in fishing, and I'm sure somewhere down deep in my psyche that's the reason I'm usually the last to retire the lure. ❋

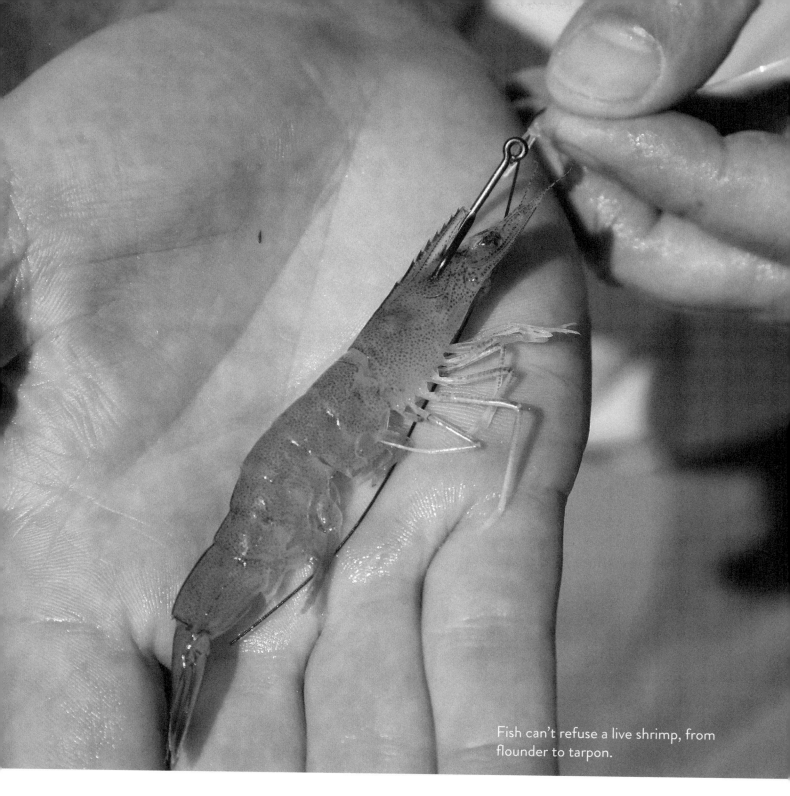

Fish can't refuse a live shrimp, from flounder to tarpon.

Chapter 9
Rigging Live Shrimp
Few offerings can beat a frisky, precision-rigged live shrimp!

The lowly shrimp may be the most commonly used bait south of the Mason-Dixon line. Aside from being fairly cheap and easy to keep alive, these prolific crustaceans rank high on the menu of many popular inshore species, including grouper, bonefish, tarpon, snook, seatrout, redfish and jacks. Here are several ways to rig a live shrimp for fishing in different situations.

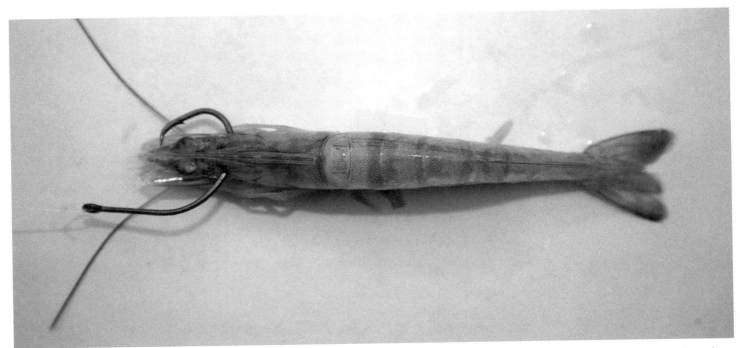

1) If you intend to drift your shrimp in the current or suspend it below a float rig or popping cork, you'll want to take advantage of its natural kicking action, which often pushes the strike button of many game fish. The best way to do this is to hook the shrimp through its carapace. However, it is important to avoid the shrimp's stomach and pancreas, which appear as two translucent dark spots. In version one, the hook is threaded crosswise through the carapace, just under the tip of the shell.

2) In version two, which will provide more casting distance and make the shrimp easier to retrieve, the hook point is threaded under the "chin" and exits through the center of the carapace, just behind the "horn" and between the vital organs. When hooked in this way, the shrimp won't live as long as it would if hooked crosswise through the carapace.

3) When casting distance is important, as it can be when trying to bait a cruising fish, it's best to hook the shrimp through the tail. This will place the heavier head section forward while reducing the chances of the shrimp tearing off on the cast. Also, removing the shrimp's tail fan will emit a scent that attracts fish. After breaking off the tail fan, thread the hook through the center of the tail until the entire shank is hidden and push the point through the underside of the tail. Now push the tail over the hook eye and knot to hide them. A baitholder-style hook will help prevent the shrimp from sliding off the hook.

4) To make a weedless casting rig for fishing in grassy areas, break off the tail fan and push the hook point all the way through the tip of the tail. Pull the shank out of the tail and invert the hook, so that the point faces the underside of the shrimp. Lastly, embed the point of the hook in the tail meat.

5) Yet another way to rig a shrimp for basic casting and drift-fishing is to run the hook through the tip of the tail, either crosswise or up through the center of the tail. The latter keeps the hook point clear of bottom snags. Many experts prefer this method because it allows the shrimp to kick freely and puts the hook in a good position for striking when a game fish eats the bait head-first. The tail fan can be left on, or removed to provide additional scent.

This monster tripletail engulfed a live shrimp pitched under a navigation buoy.

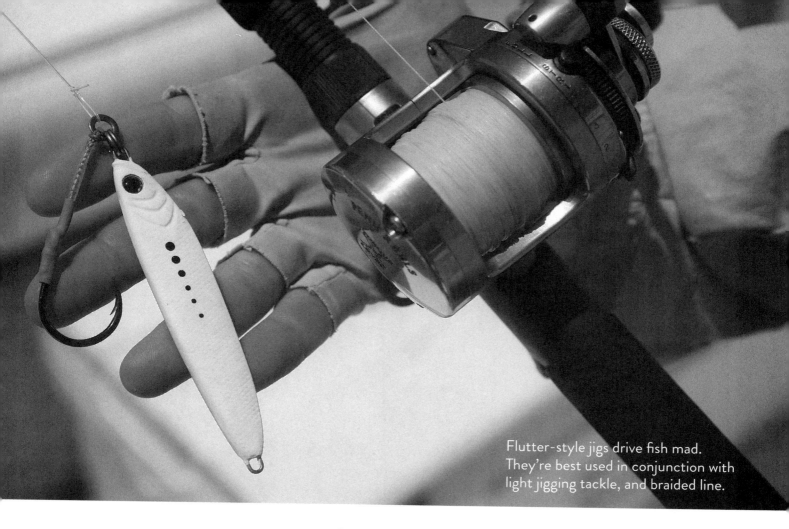

Flutter-style jigs drive fish mad. They're best used in conjunction with light jigging tackle, and braided line.

Chapter 10
Flatter 'Em with Flutter
Flutter-jig for flat out action!

Captain Mark Schmidt hit the nail on the head, when questioned on the "hype" over flutter-style jigs. "It shows the fish something different, and provokes a reaction," quipped the veteran light tackle Key West guide. Schmidt then lent an example, where he was fishing for mangrove snapper alongside another boat using live bait. "On that particular day, I was out-fishing that boat three-to-one with a-ounce flutter-style jig," says Schmidt. "That's how hot these things can be, and I've many more examples where they've really stood out and put fish in boat." More later!

Flutter style jigs have caught countless numbers fish since they've come onto the market, ranging from inshore species such as striped bass, bluefish, snappers and groupers to offshore warriors the likes of bluefin and yellowfin tuna, wahoo and dolphin. Nearly everything eats them, and you don't have to be a seasoned veteran to fool fish with them. Compared with traditional jigs, such as the arrow-head and deep jig designs, which descend straight and rapidly through the water column, flutter-style jigs have an inherent, radical action coupled with a slightly slower and wandering descent; they're designed to imitate an injured or frantically fleeing baitfish scrambling in confused directions. This type

of action evokes an instinctive "kill" response from game fish, even from those which aren't necessarily hungry.

With traditional jigging, it's the angler who must impart the action and continually "dial it in" until the fish respond; success is basically 90-percent angler skill and 10-percent jig. With flutter style jigging, conversely, it's basically 90-percent jig and 10-percent angler skill; that's how "dialed in" these lures come. This is a result of their fatter, wider and often slightly contorted bodies – which catch water and increase resistance when descending through the water column, and precision weight distribution - whether it's top or bottom heavy, or offset somewhere in between those extremes. These factors all combine to produce their wild, radical and erratic "fluttering" actions; when fish are present, anglers merely need to get a flutter-style jig into the zone, whip the rod, and let its actions elicit strikes. They're the "great equalizers" in the deep-jigging world.

Schmidt On The Stand

Despite their effectiveness, there is still concern over choosing the "right" one, whether color makes a difference, and how to work them. Captain Mark Schmidt says choosing the "right" flutter-style jig is no different than selecting a traditional deep jig. "I like to pick the lightest flutter-jig that I can still hold bottom with and fish for grouper and snapper," says Schmidt. "If my jig stays on bottom for only a few seconds before drifting up the water column - where the amberjack are - I switch to a heavier one. When fishing shallow wrecks and rock

Light, yet stout rods and small conventional reels filled with braided line make ideal "flutter-jigging" outfits. The objective is to whip the rod up, and then instantly throw slack in the line by quickly lowering the rod tip to the water, which enables the jig to "flutter" and react like an injured baitfish scurrying for its life.

DOWN, AND EVEN OUT!

Flutter style jigs are not just intended to be fished horizontally. They're extremely potent in casting situations. For example, I keep a pair of light spinning outfits (20-pound test braided line and 30-pound test fluorocarbon leaders) rigged with 1-ounce to 1-3/4-ounce flutter-style jigs (more specifically, Williamson Gyro Jigs). When we see small tunas, like blackfins and yellowfins, busting under birds, we'll ease close to the action, and make a long cast (braided line enables this) into the ruckus. Rarely does it take more than a few cranks to hook-up. The flutter jigs are basically the same size of the small bait the tuna are pushing up, and recreate nearly the same fleeing actions. I'll also use these smaller jigs for breaking Spanish and Cero mackerel, and even bonito – when we just want something to pull on. The same works for bluefish, striped bass, tarpon, etc.

piles between 25 and 30 feet of water, I prefer the 1-1/2 and 2-ounce flutter jigs - if they hold bottom well. And for small snapper like those leery mangroves, I'll even scale down to a 1/2-ounce jig, just like I did that day in the boat where I out-fished anglers using live bait.

"For grouper, snapper and amberjack on wrecks in 180-feet or more, I first try getting down with a 2-1/2-ounce jig, but will go as heavy as 5-ounces if current and drift require it. If the current is really cooking, I'll select a more streamlined jig, which cuts through the water with less resistance and gets down faster."

As for "hot" colors, Schmidt's extensive flutter jigging experience has taught him one important thing: "It's not so much about picking the right color as it is choosing a jig with some prominent glow paint in its pattern," says Schmidt. "This is so true in deep water, where I believe

the glow provides for a more visual target. Given a choice between, say, a flutter jig with natural colors and one with natural colors but with some glow features in the paint, I'm picking the one containing the glow. It's like the old deep-jigging days when we tipped our lead heads with a glow worm or glow tail. There's just something about "glow" that these fish like".

Mark Schmidt also has at least one rod rigged with a flutter-style jig, no matter what he's fishing for. "One April, we were on a Gulf wreck catching bait and looking for permit," says Schmidt. "I handed my customer a flutter-jigging outfit and told him to go "prospecting"; he immediately began catching kingfish we didn't know were there! So, the flutter jig sees a lot of action on my boat, even when it's not our primary tactic."

The elongated, thick bodies of flutter style jigs yield an erratic, "wobbling"-type of action. Many designs even rely on offset weight points along their bodies, for more intense actions. Picture here is the Williamson Raku jig. Note the independent body, which promotes even more of a "wobbling" action.

Southwest Florida Flutter-Meister

Darren Blum, an accomplished Southwest Florida-based offshore and bottom-fishing specialist, is a big proponent of flutter-jigging. "Off Sarasota, it's a long run offshore to reach deep water, but the fishing out here can be amazing," says Blum. "We flutter jig for groupers and snappers over Swiss cheese bottom, rockpiles and wrecks, and we're also set to pitch them at pelagics – like Mahi, blackfins, kingfish and wahoo. For me, they're most effective out beyond 120-feet of water. I prefer the "natural" patterns – like mackerel or even mullet, in waters up to 200 feet deep. But beyond that, it's strictly glow-patterns or pink for us, as they get bit the most. As far as dialing in on the best weight, a 4-1/2-ounce jig is good overall, yet sometimes I'll bump up to 6-1/2-ounces when the drift or current is too fast. And when a fast current or drift becomes a real issue, I'll switch to a pencil-style speed jig, to reach and hold bottom faster and easier. Remember, I'm referring to deep water flutter-jigging here."

Blum also revealed his most potent flutter jig action - the "vertical walk-the-dog". That is, after the jig reaches bottom, he'll let it settle for two or three seconds. He then jigs it upwards and lets it descend back to bottom - keeping within 15 feet of the bottom. He repeats this tactic a half-dozen times. "This makes the jig appear as if it's a wounded baitfish," says Blum. Then, after jigging near the bottom, he'll continue the vertical walk-the-dog beat right back to the boat, but now in a quicker, more radical fashion than the initial half-dozen strokes. "And this makes the jig appear more like a fleeing baitfish", says Blum. His initial effort focuses on groupers and snappers, while the effort back to the boat is intended for jacks, kings, wahoo, blackfins and dolphin. Blum believes that if a fish isn't turned on by the "wounded" action, the "fleeing" action just might do the trick, and vice-versa.

Blum was quick to point out that when flutter jigging, he prefers a vigorous action. He jerks the rod up hard and rapidly, and only reels to catch up with the slack line. It's the rod that is "lifting" the lure up, and not the reeling. Because of the size of some of these offshore bottom fish, especially those around wrecks, he uses 80-pound test braided line and a 20-foot top-shot of 80-pound test fluorocarbon. His jigging rods carry a minimum rating of 80-pound test.

When offshore trolling, Blum keeps handy spin tackle spooled with 50-pound braid and rigged with flutter jigs on 60-pound test fluorocarbon leaders. "We keep these ready, should we see busting pelagics – like tuna," says Blum. "But if we see an attractive piece of structure on the fishfinder, we'll mark it and circle back around. Then, when we're back on top of the find, we'll pause above it for a minute or so, put a couple anglers in the bow, and have them drop the flutter jigs. We've caught impressive bottom fish this way and acquired new spots. I don't think there's a snapper or grouper I haven't caught on these jigs. I've taken mangroves, true reds, scamps, yellow-eyes, snowies, gags, blacks, Warsaw and even trigger fish!".

Global In Concept

Both the general concept and tactics used by both Schmidt and Blum apply wherever flutter-jigging is practiced, whether it's in the inshore and offshore waters of the northeast, mid-Atlantic, Southeast, Gulf of Mexico and the Pacific. I've "flutter-jigged" with good success on black sea bass off Buzzard's

FLUTTER-JIGGING 101

1.) Braided line is a must, as its thin diameter cuts through the water better than a monofilament of the same breaking strength. This enables lighter jigs to reach and hold bottom better. Plus, braid telegraphs the "feel and action" of the jig, and even the subtlest strike. What's more, there's no stretch, so positive hook-ups soar – especially with deep bottom fish.

2.) Use small conventional reels and the new generation of light, yet strong, jigging and casting rods. Flutter-jigging requires elbow grease, and lightweight tackle eliminates fatigue.

3.) Even though a flutter jig still has a solid eye ring to tie to, still use an overhand loop knot to join leader to lure. This will provide even a bit more freedom for the jig to "dance", and maximize its action.

4.) A single hook has been proving to be just as effective as a dual set-up. Plus, it's easier on fish being released and the angler doing the un-hooking duties.

5.) Speaking of hooks, an increasing number of anglers have been replacing the standard J-style hook with an in-line circle hook, and discovering better hook-up and landing results.

6.) Make sure a swivel is incorporated into the flutter-jig system. This will alleviate line twist caused by the wild, erratic actions of the jig, particularly when used in conjunction with spin tackle.

7.) Avoid tying the leader to a split eye ring, as there's a real risk of the leader slipping through the ring when jigging or playing a fish, and losing your jig and fish.

Bay, Massachusetts, bluefish and striped bass off Connecticut, amberjack from Virginia Beach down through Key West, and tuna and wahoo off South Florida, the Bahamas, and Gulf of Mexico. Of course, there will be little subtleties involved when being species-specific - including leader selection, and also depending upon the environment one is fishing in – i.e. channels, bays, inlets/passes, reefs, wrecks, canyons and under bait and birds.

When fishing for toothy pelagics, for example, I'll still stick with a fluorocarbon leader – unless the fish are so solid they're not deterred by a light (38 to 40-pound test) single strand wire leader. However, I'll change my retrieve. When dropping under floating debris and under dolphin schools for wahoo, I'll let the flutter jig fall about 100-feet. I'll then engage the drag and retrieve the jig as quickly and as straight as possible, where it appears like a healthy bait racing for the surface. So, if a wahoo strikes, it will hopefully "catch" the flutter jig below its head, and miss the fluorocarbon leader. If the jig were whipped in traditional fashion, a fish will likely strike on the fall. And that's when the jig is falling ahead of the leader. And when that happens, the fish will catch the jig and leader on the bite – and you've just lost both!

Regardless of species, two things should remain foremost when selecting or rigging a flutter-style jig. Since line twist can become an issue, due to their inherent erratic actions, a swivel should be incorporated into the system – whether it's joining the leader to the fishing line, or on the jig itself. This is especially true when used in conjunction with spin tackle. A swivel will alleviate line twist. Equally important, make sure the jig has (or incorporate into it) a solid eye ring. Avoid tying your line directly to the split ring eye, as stories continue to mount on how a quality fish was lost when the fishing line slid into the split ring, and eventually off of it.

As mentioned earlier, it's hard not to score with flutter-jigs, no matter the species or geography. Once you try them over the course of several trips, and review your score cards, you'll be wondering why you didn't jump on the flutter-jig band wagon a long time ago! ✳

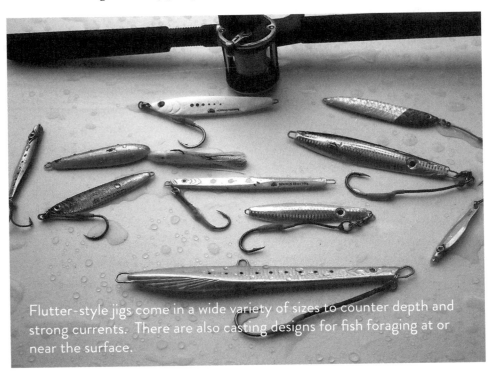

Flutter-style jigs come in a wide variety of sizes to counter depth and strong currents. There are also casting designs for fish foraging at or near the surface.

Dave Morel takes the fight right to a big Dusky shark he hooked off Bimini. Thanks to a functional and well adjusted rod belt and harness combination, he whipped the big fish in an impressively quick fashion.

Chapter 11
Harnessed to Win!
Buckle up and use leverage to defeat big fish!

It had become a frustrating deal for SWS Publisher Dave Morel, Chris Megan, Penn's John Bartow, and me. We were into a school of tuna 30 miles from Bimini, but sharks kept picking off nearly every one we hooked. Suddenly, as if to add insult to injury, this huge Dusky appeared alongside the MARC VI, eerily eye-balling us. This shark was big enough to impress even Dave and Chris – both staunch New England shark fanatics. Yet, what Dave asked me to do next bordered on the unthinkable, at least for a southern Florida offshore angler!

Sensing I was about to say: "It's time to head for the barn", and write this spot off to the sharks, Dave asked if he could catch the big Dusky. I was

speechless, initially. For most southern Florida offshore anglers it would have had to be a painfully slow day for us to bait a shark – unless, of course, it was a Mako. I didn't want to mess with the shark, so I side-stepped the issue for a bit - but Dave pressed on. Understanding job security, I gave in to Dave's third request and told him to fetch the shark rig out of my tackle bag. We attached the cable rig to a Penn 50-International stand-up outfit and eventually hand-fed a whole bonito to the monster - right alongside the boat!

Dave looked as happy as a middle-aged man who just purchased a new Corvette, as the shark ran off 50-pound test line, while he held on. We now

faced another dilemma. The sun was hanging low, and we had to be back at Bimini Sands for a 7:00 p.m. func-tion (which we never made, thanks to Dave and that shark!). I told Dave to take the fight to the shark and end it soon, one way or the other. For this, he donned a Black Magic Equalizer Rod Belt, and an AFTCO MaxForce stand-up harness, and really pressured the beast - like the true pro he is. In less than an hour, we leadered the monster shark, clipped the cable near the hook, and called it a long day!

Harness Your Power
A combination rod belt and harness - whether it's a shoulder or kidney design, enables an angler to apply

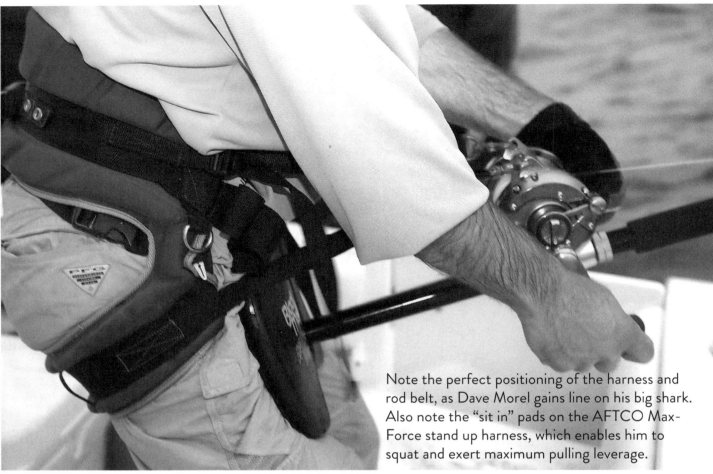

Note the perfect positioning of the harness and rod belt, as Dave Morel gains line on his big shark. Also note the "sit in" pads on the AFTCO Max-Force stand up harness, which enables him to squat and exert maximum pulling leverage.

and maintain an incredible amount of pressure throughout the duration of a fight – much more so than simply standing up and fighting a big game fish without this equipment. They're the difference between beating a fish quickly, or prolonging the fight and increasing the odds of losing the fish due to angler fatigue, terminal tackle failure, or predation by sharks. Credit goes to the additional leverage and pulling power these set-ups provide, by enabling an angler to tax their upper back and shoulders (shoulder harness) or lower back and leg muscles (kidney-style harness), rather than just stand flat-footed and use just their arms. Also, during a long fight, a good belt and harness combo lets anglers use certain muscles and rest certain muscles, to pace themselves while not lessening the pressuring on the fish.

Yet, with all the various types of belts and harnesses on the market, se-lecting the proper one for your type of fishing can be intimidating, especially for those relatively new to offshore stand-up fishing.

Rick's Rules

Rick Mola is an ardent canyon angler and owner of Fisherman's World tackle center in Norwalk, Connecticut (www.fishermansworld.net). Although his shop is stocked to catch everything from fluke to broadbill swordfish, Mola outfits an impressively large number of canyon-bound boats. When questioned on how to choose the best rod belt and harness set up, he quickly stated that it comes down to custom fitting each individual angler, and what "feels right" to them . "For example, we sell a lot of 50W reels filled with 80-pound test line and stand-up rods equipped with short, AFTCO curved butt rods" says Mola. "This is a prominent canyon

set-up now, thanks to the resurgence of swordfish. So, anglers are out there primarily chunking for tuna, but also encountering sharks and swordfish. Buying this style of outfit, I may have one angler who is five-feet, two-inches tall, and another who might be six-feet, five-inches tall, and both will be looking for the right belt and harness set-up to handle that outfit, and, naturally, the equipment will vary with their comfort levels."

For rod belts, Mola says to choose a model that is wide and large enough to efficiently redistribute the torque and pressure from that outfit and fight to across one's thighs. For a stand-up outfit, the rod belt must be positioned low to achieve maximum leverage, to where it covers both groin and upper thighs. "The wider-based rod belts are much more adequate at doing this, over the lighter, smaller ones," says Mola. "Smaller belts are fine for light tackle fishing, but when you step up to serious stand-up gear, they simply can't spread that pressure out across a broader area of your thighs. And then what happens, you end up being uncomfortable during the fight and even bruising yourself. So, it's not worth saving a few extra dollars at the expense of becoming black-and-blue, and not fighting the good fight."

Once the fighting belt and respective harness have been selected, Mola will have his clients don the gear. He'll then hand them a 50-pound class stand-up outfit, and proceed to make the necessary adjustments for their comfort and fighting efficiency – and this is accomplished by him applying 20-pounds of pressure on the rod. "If they begin to stumble about or feel uncomfortable, we'll try different harnesses and belt combinations and adjustments until they can comfortably stand flat-footed and handle the pulling power," claims Mola.

"Another typical situation is that a boat usually has just one, or maybe two belts and harness combos," says Mola". "And when a big fish is hooked, that belt and harness likely hasn't been adjusted properly for the angler. Therefore, they fumble about trying to adjust it on the spot, which interferes with the angler's rhythm. And chances are once it is adjusted, it could have been fine-tuned even more, had it been done earlier at the dock. That's why it's so important for serious anglers to have their own personal equipment dialed in specifically for them."

Shoulder vs. Kidney

Whether to opt for a shoulder-style or kidney-style harness is personal preference. However, as a general rule, a rod belt/shoulder harness set-up is best suited for lighter stand-up tackle, i.e. 20-pound, 30-pound- and 50-pound

class. This will enable an angler to use their upper back and shoulders to pressure a fish. And during a long fight, the angler can give their back and shoulder muscles a break by pumping with their arms, and vice-versa. I've used this set-up quite a bit, and it really lends an advantage when playing out yellowfin tuna on 30-pound class and even blue marlin on 50-pound class gear.

I prefer to adjust the shoulder harness to where the rod is nearly upright enough to where I can reach straight out with my left arm and grasp its upper fore grip. It's sort of like an imaginary upside-down "triangle", where the rod gimbal and belt is the point, my body and the rod making up the sides, and my outstretched arm on top, connecting my body to the rod, representing the base. With this

A well fitted- harness/rod belt set-up enabled Dave Morel to bring this monster Dusky shark alongside the MARC VI.

set-up, I merely bow a bit to reel in line, and straighten back up to pump the fish. And, as mentioned earlier, should I need to rest those upper back and shoulder muscles, I simply reach out, grasp the rod's upper fore grip and pump and wind using my arms.

Aboard my boat, I also carry an AFTCO MaxForce stand up harness, which is what we put Dave Morel into for that shark battle. Although this is a great set up for light tackle as well, I prefer it for 50- and 80-pound class stand-up gear; some anglers use it with 130-pound class gear. The advantage of this harness style, when used in conjunction with the appropriate rod belt, is that one can exert

pressure from not only the lower back region, but also from the hips and upper thighs; you basically squat and use your weight to exert maximum pulling leverage. What's more, the sit in pads are extremely comfortable.

When a fish runs, I prefer keeping my left hand over the face of the reel, and my other hand on the reel handle (with both shoulder and kidney designs). The arc in the rod from the properly adjusted harness and rod belt will maintain steep pressure on the fish, while I simply relax my arms, and wait to counter. When it's time to gain ground, I'll keep my left hand over the reel and level wind as I lean forward to reclaim line. Also, keeping my hand over the reel will enable me to stop the rod from snapping back and hitting my face, should the hook pull or line part while pumping the fish. To pump up the fish, I'll squat backwards into the harness, lifting the rod.

Just how effective this type of pressure can be on a fish, when executed properly, was showcased by Dave Morel on that shark. He settled into a fast-paced, high-pressure pace that began taking its toll on the shark. Before he suited up in the belt and harness, he couldn't do much

with the fish. Yes, Dave was breaking a sweat and working hard, but he beat a very large predator on a 50-pound stand-up outfit in relatively quick time.

Safety First

Despite the fun and excitement of slugging it out with a powerful, big game fish, there's an inherent danger involved in being strapped into a harness. Rick Mola contends that a mate or second person should stay with the angler throughout the entire fight, standing by to grab them should they slip or lose balance (many harnesses have safety handles on the back, for this very purpose). This is especially so when it's rough and aboard a boat with low gunwales. Mola also recommends a safety line on all big game outfits. Should the unthinkable occur, the restraint will keep all within quick reach of help. Also, some of the harnesses have release clips that quickly attach to and detach from a reel, and it's good sense to keep a knife or cutting tool on you (angler).

It's not only going overboard that concerns me, but also the angler falling backwards and hitting their head, back or ribs on a rocket launcher, chair or gunwale, should the line part while they're pressuring the fish. That's why I stood directly behind Dave Morel, and had Chris Megan take my place when I needed to take the wheel. With us standing over him, Dave was not going to go overboard, or fall back into the cockpit and injure himself.

No doubt, when there's a tough fight on tap, nothing helps to make short work of a big, powerful, stubborn fish than a good angler in a well-matched, comfortable and efficient rod belt and harness set-up. I saw the scenario play out yet once again off Bimini this past summer. So did Dave Morel. ✳

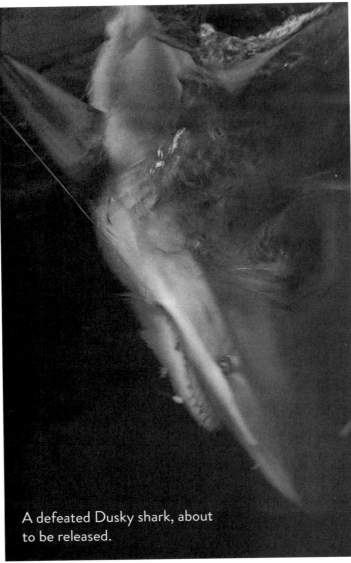

A defeated Dusky shark, about to be released.

Strong currents associated with full- and new-moon tides can alter the feeding patterns of fish.

Chapter 12

Playing the Tides

How tide determines where and when fish will feed

Few things influence the feeding patterns of inshore fish as strongly as tide. Serious fishermen live by the tides, which flush out and replenish a body of water with oxygen, nutrients, bait and game fish. Experience and careful observation have taught them where their favorite target species will feed during various stages of the tide, and they can predict with impressive accuracy where these fish will relocate when subjected to higher or lower tides. For these pros, catching fish becomes a matter of setting up at the right spots during the right stages of a tide.

Timing the tide was the key to success on a recent trip to western Long Island Sound off Norwalk, Connecticut. I had joined Rick Mola, owner of Fisherman's World Tackle Center in South Norwalk, to diamond-jig for the big bluefish that invade the region during late fall and early winter. Because the moon was full, Mola knew that the final stages of the outgoing tide would be prime for jigging the ledges and humps we planned to fish. This tide stage happened to occur late in the afternoon.

We left the dock at noon, despite Mola's prediction that the fish

wouldn't show up until the final hour or so of daylight. We didn't mark a single fish on the depthsounder for most of the afternoon, but then, during the final hour of that big, 8-foot outgoing tide, the area came alive with countless 10- to 15-pound blues!

Spring and Neap Tides

Tide, it should be noted, is the vertical rise and fall of the water level, and should not be confused with current (the horizontal flow of water), although the two are inextricably linked. Tides are the result of the gravitation

Tides play an important role in the lives of game fish by flushing out and replenishing oxygen, nutrients and baitfish in a body of water.

and centrifugal forces exerted by the moon as it rotates around the earth and, to a smaller degree, the sun. When the moon and sun are in alignment, their combined gravitational force increases the range of the tides. These are known as "spring tides," and they occur around the full and new moons. Spring tides yield the highest high tides and lowest low tides within the monthly cycle. In contrast, when the moon and sun are at right angles to each other, their gravitational forces counteract each other and reduce the tidal range. These are called "neap tides," and they occur during the moon's first and third quarters.

If the moon was stationary and did not rotate around the earth, we would have two high tides and two low tides precisely every 24 hours. However, since the moon does rotate around the earth, and appears over the same place on earth approximately 50 minutes later each day, we see two high tides and two low tides every 24 hours and 50 minutes. This is why a specific tide stage is approximately 50 minutes later each day. For instance, if you discovered that the beginning of an incoming tide at sunrise was ideal for producing seatrout over a certain grass flat, the exact tidal stage would occur roughly 50 minutes later with each passing day.

Outside Influences

It should be noted that tides also are affected by the topography of the coast. That's why tides can vary by 15 minutes or more at different spots along the same stretch of coastline. Other factors can affect the tide and its im-

pact on fishing. For example, an outgoing tide in an estuary can be slowed to some degree by a strong opposing wind. The wind can actually overpower the tide and prevent the water from leaving the system. In this case, if you were waiting on the final hour of an outgoing tide to concentrate fish in the feeder creeks or channels, you just might discover that the wind was holding back enough water to keep them spread throughout the shallows.

Conversely, a hard wind blowing in the same direction as the outgoing tide can force water out of an estuary at a faster pace. If you didn't factor this in, you could arrive at your hot spot and find that you missed the best stage of the tide. In very shallow estuaries or flats, you might not find any water at all!

The speed at which the tide rises and falls is not constant, and neither is the velocity of a tidal current as it enters and leaves a particular area. The rise or fall of the water begins and ends gradually, and peaks in the middle of the cycle. This means that an area will experience stronger tidal currents during the middle of the tide as opposed to the beginning and end.

Tide and Location

The velocity of a tidal current also

increases as water is forced through shallow or narrow passages, such as bars or inets. This can influence where fish will take up station to feed. For example, if snook typically stack up along the jetties to forage on bait washing out of an inlet or pass during the calmer stages of an outgoing tide, the peak of the tide might prompt these same fish to relocate along the deep side of a ledge or around the backside of the jetties, where eddies form and trap bait and the current is not as strong. Fish will seek out spots where they can lie in wait to ambush prey without having to fight the full velocity of the current.

Conversely, a higher volume of water moving into an area enables bait and game fish to spread out over the shallows or into heavy vegetation, making them a challenge to reach by boat or with a bait or lure. Certain pockets, ledges and bars that usually hold fish during the milder, incoming stages of a neap tide could possibly be void of them during high spring tides.

What all this means to fishermen is that it's critical to take note of the specific feeding stations of game fish during various stages of a tide. For example, had my Norwalk bluefish trip taken place one week earlier,

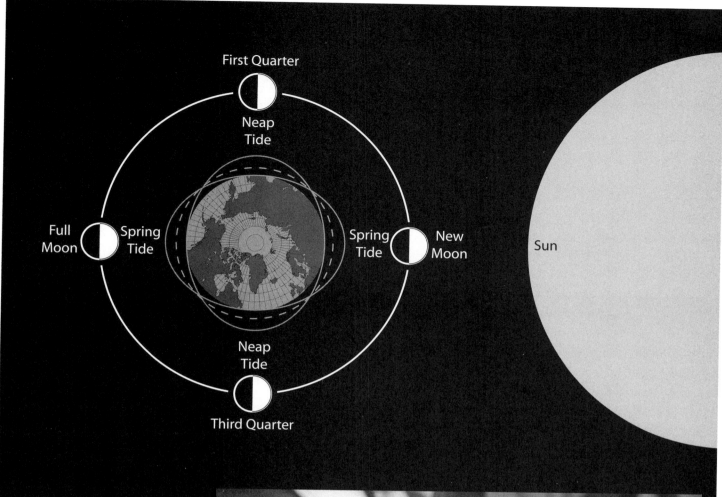

when 6 foot tides were the norm, the prime time for fishing the ledges would have been during the middle of the outgoing tide. Depending on the stage of the tide and the velocity of the tidal current, it's common for fish to drop back, move aside or retreat to deeper holes to counter swift-moving water. Spring tides present even more of a challenge, since the increased volume of water tends to broaden the playing field.

Offshore Tides

Tides also affect action with offshore species. For example, bottom fishing for grouper and snapper excels when the tide creates a moderately strong current, which moves bait and promotes effective chumming.

Some structure-oriented fish, such as blackfish, often take advantage of the slower stages of a tide to feed. The lesser stages of a tide also enable anglers to effectively fish these structures.

Tides also affect the feeding patterns of offshore game fish. Wahoo are notorious for feeding heavily around the final stages of an outgoing tide and initial stages of an incoming tide.

This can be caused by a tide change in some areas. We know that a full or new moon tide tends to produce stronger currents, which can influence bottom fishing. In many cases, a moderate to strong flow of water often requires more weight to hold bottom and more thought on how to chum effectively over structure, yet the fishing can be sensational. Also, I've experienced many instances when weaker tides have resulted in minimal water flow, which has slowed the fishing.

When king mackerel chase bait along the beaches, tides have a major influence on where they'll be. For example, at certain times of the year, the tide line or rips that are formed by outgoing inshore water meeting clean ocean water are patrolled by big king mackerel, as well as Spanish mackerel, tarpon, cobia, bull redfish and jack crevalle. These fish are seeking the bait carried out with the tide. Anglers fish along these tide lines and rips as they progress offshore from the inlet or pass, and again as they approach the channels ahead of clean, incoming ocean water.

Throughout South Florida, the Bahamas and other areas where deep water lies close to shore, wahoo tend to feed heavily during the last hour of the outgoing tide and first hour of the incoming tide. There-

fore, serious wahoo anglers plan their arrival at certain hot spots during these stages of the tide, regardless of whether it's 7:00 a.m. or 3:00 p.m.

Not long ago, a few friends and I set forth to catch wahoo off Boca Raton, Florida. With the last hour of the outgoing tide occurring around 1:00 p.m., the captain elected not to concentrate on wahoo until then. Instead, we trolled well offshore for dolphin before returning to the wahoo grounds a little after noon. As anticipated, the bite was on and we ended up boating a hefty 'hoo.

Understanding how tides

influence the various species you fish for isn't a quick process. It has taken some of the best guides years to get a solid grip on where the fish will be on a certain tide stage and how other factors such as barometric pressure, cold fronts, wind and major tide swings influence their movements and behavior. There's no substitute for noting the tide stage and location when you uncover good fishing, as well as the weather. In time, you'll have a valuable playbook that will tell you where to fish throughout the day. When you have a handle on the tides, catching fish becomes a lot easier! ❋

Leverage the boat's throttle to hold over a school of fish or good piece of bottom, and to maintain slight headway to tow your baits into a new zone.

Chapter 13
Power-Drifting Fishing Tactics
Stem the current and catch more fish

Those who regularly drop anchor or power-drift over structure in pursuit of bottomfish know all too well that if we're off our mark by as little as several feet, we'll miss the bite. Successful bottomfishing is an intricate game interweaving current, wind, structure, depth, fish habits and precise positioning: Identify where the fish are stacking, get your baits down into that zone, and come home a winner.

Power drifting is a common tactic over deep structure and wrecks in situations where anchoring would prove impractical - or monumental. It basically requires the helmsman to use the boat power to stem a current and/or hold into a wind and remain over a precise piece of bottom long enough to jig or soak baits around it. It's downright effective on all types of bottomfish, and even pelagics.

As elementary as it sounds, the tactic still perplexes many. How do you position the boat right on top of that spot long enough to probe for fish? How do you fish multiple lines and avoid tangles? And when the wind or current become a factor, how do you keep from sliding off your mark? With all of the scenarios above in play, setting up for an effective drift can require a little bit of strategizing.

Even for inshore fish, like fluke, power-drifting is a winning tactic.

Battle Plan

One of Capt. Bouncer Smith's many specialties is power drifting over deep wrecks, ledges, humps and other prominent structures off Miami, where he catches grouper, snapper, cobia, amberjack, African pompano, kingfish, and even the occasional wahoo and sailfish. He's a master of this game and has simplified the process and identified the keys to successful power drifting.

Given the advancements in marine electronics, locating and sizing up a wreck or bottom structure has never been easier. Smith recommends making a north-south pass over the structure, marking a waypoint at each end. Then he advises making another pass over the structure, this time east to west and once again marking the waypoint at both ends. "So now you have four waypoints that outline the wreck," says Smith. "With the wreck marked clearly on your chart plotter, you know precisely where it is and

When schools of fish, like this blue-fish, are lighting up on the fishfinder, and you're faced with a fast drift, use the boat's power to hold over the active area - and score!

where your boat is in relationship to that structure."

"You should also watch your fish finder during your passes over the wreck and take note where the fish are concentrated," he says. "In our area grouper tend to station upstream of a wreck, the mutton snapper behind or downstream, mangroves and yellowtail on top, and cobia and amberjack above and in front of a wreck."

Once the structure, as well as where the fish are holding, is identified on the plotter, consider how wind and current will influence your positioning over that spot. Line up the waypoint you plan to fish and initially position yourself well ahead of the wreck. As the boat drifts back to the wreck, you'll get a good idea of how to compensate to remain above the target.

Marching Orders

"Wind will be the biggest factor in power drifting, and with an outboard boat, you must keep stern to the wind to maintain control," says Smith. "Think of the

Rigging tips: The Feel Deal

Staying in contact with your bottom bait will put more fish in the box. Braid telegraphs the subtle rolls of the sinker over bottom and strikes right up the line to the angler, giving him the advantage of knowing exactly what is happening down below. It is a big plus for bottomfishing. Here are five tips that will help you keep in touch with your bottom baits:

- Use braided line and low-stretch fluorocarbon leaders to monitor your baits.
- Always use the lightest sinker to hold bottom, as heavy weights diminish your ability to detect subtle strikes.
- Always keep a slightly taut line to feel the action of your bait.
- Always strive to feel the sinker on or near the bottom. This is done by free-spooling until the sinker hits bottom and then taking a turn or two on the reel handle to remove slack.
- Watch the rod tip, as it will reveal the slightest tap on the line.

Power drifting works well on tuna, like this yellowfin, when using live baits and also chunking.

zones. You might even consider using a different bait on that lighter outfit so it will also appeal to different species."

And if working two bottom baits isn't enough, Smith recommends adding a vertical jig to the mix and free-lining a surface bait for pelagics foraging in the water column.

Power drifting also offers anglers mobility. Hook into a large fish and you can power away with it, where remaining stationary might result in a cutoff.

engine as a flagpole and the boat as the flag. Therefore, seas permitting, power-drift in reverse over the structure for the most control and fishing time over a spot. Use enough reverse throttle to hold your position and keep the fishing lines nearly vertical.

"Once you're in position, keeping everyone fishing and tangle-free also requires some thought. Braided line is a must for this style of fishing, due to its minimal resistance. Furthermore, its lack of stretch promotes more solid hookups. Plus, it's just tough stuff and great for fishing around structure."

Lock and Load

The next factor involves using just enough weight to reach and remain in contact with bottom. "To keep lines from tangling in a power-drifting situation, one rod should have a lighter weight than the others," says Smith. "Just a couple less ounces of

weight on one outfit could make a big difference. The line with the lighter weight will be subject to more blow-back, which will position the line and its bait farther back than the line and bait on the outfit with the heavier weight. Both baits will be fishing in different

Power drifting produces over both deep and shallow structure, such as inlet ledges and rock piles. Master the proper boat handling and bait deployment, and your final challenge just might be trying to muscle a trophy fish away from its home. ✳

Power-drifting and holding over a wreck or prime piece of bottom structure allows those structures to be thoroughly fished, whether you're live-baiting, jigging or soaking baits on bottom. This porgy was captured off a deep bottom peak.

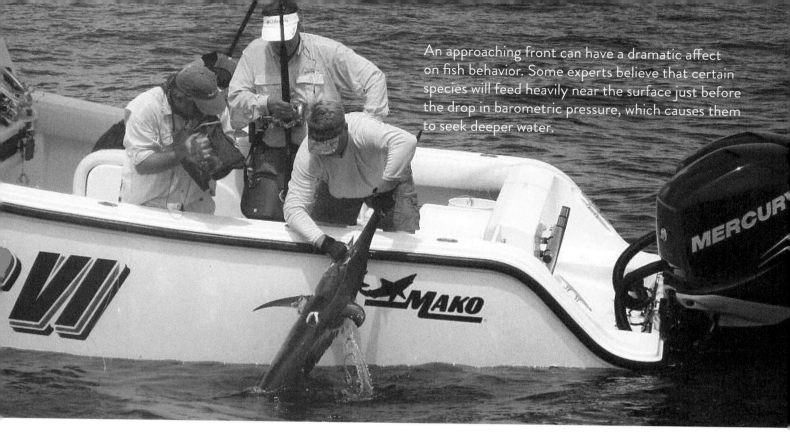

An approaching front can have a dramatic affect on fish behavior. Some experts believe that certain species will feed heavily near the surface just before the drop in barometric pressure, which causes them to seek deeper water.

Chapter 14
Fishing by the Barometer
Find out how barometric pressure influences fish behavior in your neighborhood!

Every angler knows that tide, water temperature, light level and moon phase can affect our fishing success, but there's another factor that often goes overlooked. Although barometric pressure can't be predicted as accurately as the other elements just mentioned, it has a major influence on fish behavior.

Think about it. How many times have you enjoyed a red-hot bite before an approaching storm or frontal system, or watched the action mysteriously shut down upon the arrival of bad weather? And how many days did it take for the fish to turn back on after the passage of that storm or front?

What Is Barometric Pressure?
According to Dr. Stephen Baig, an oceanographer at NOAA's Hurricane Center in Miami, barometric pressure

is defined as the weight or mass of an entire air column on a unit of surface area at sea level. It is instrumental in weather observations, since its fluctuation indicates the movement of weather fronts and systems.

Liquid mercury (Hg) is commonly used in a barometer to measure air-pressure changes in inches (in.). "Imagine a U-shaped tube," says Dr. Baig. "At one end is liquid mercury, whereas the other end is open to the atmosphere. When the air pressure rises, it pushes the mercury higher. When the air pressure drops, so does the mercury level."

Atmospheric pressure can also be measured in millibars (mb), with a "bar" being roughly equivalent to one atmosphere of pressure (one atmosphere equals 1.01325 bars). One bar is equivalent to 29.6 in. Hg.

A barometer reading of 30 inches (Hg) is considered normal. Strong high pressure could register as high as 30.70 inches, whereas low pressure associated with a hurricane can dip below 27.30 inches (Hurricane Andrew had a measured surface pressure of 27.23 just before its landfall in Miami Dade County).

According to Dr. Baig, a barometer reading of 30.71 (1040 millibars) is a typical winter reading for a high-pressure, cold-air cell moving out of northern Canada, compared to the typical average annual pressure of 29.7 (1013 millibars) in Miami.

As a very general rule, approaching weather systems — such as cold and warm fronts, tropical waves and rain — are usually associated with low atmospheric pressure. Conversely, high atmospheric pressure usually arrives after the passage of such a

Fish with large swim bladders, such as striped bass, may experience discomfort during periods of low pressure, causing them to lay low and limit activity until high pressure returns. This could explain the famous "east is least" wind phenomenon experienced by bass fishermen.

weather system. When high pressure settles over an area, it often means bright days and relatively calm seas.

Affects on Fish

All this is very interesting, of course, but how does barometric pressure affect fish? To find out, I consulted Spud Woodward, Assistant Director for the Georgia Department of Natural Resources Coastal Resources Division and an avid king mackerel and red drum fisherman. While Woodward admits that there's no definitive

air bladder, and well in advance of humans. "Fish that have small air bladders, such as kings, Spanish mackerel, wahoo and dolphin, aren't as affected by barometric changes as those with large bladders, such as trout, redfish, tarpon, grouper and snapper," he says. "That's because fish with small bladders have a body density that's closer to that of the surrounding water. They don't sense the pressure changes as dramatically, so their comfort levels aren't drastically altered. However, many things they eat have air bladders,

squeezing their bladders, the bladders expand a bit. When their bladders expand, fish become uncomfortable. They relieve their discomfort by moving lower in the water column or by absorbing extra gas in their bladders. Because of the anatomical and physiological stresses exerted on them, they're not worried about eating. They're more concerned with trying to find a depth where they can stabilize their bladder pressure and feel good. Some species will settle to the bottom and ride out the change near structure. Fortunately for the fish — and

According to Woodward, fish are much more comfortable when there's stable high pressure, and tend to feed actively most anywhere within the water column.

answer for how a rising or falling barometer affects fish behavior, he has some thoughts based on his decades of marine research and some 15 years of tournament fishing.

According to Woodward, a fish senses pressure changes through its

and that alone could have a big impact on where you might find them and how they'll behave.

"Fish with large bladders quickly sense when the air pressure is dropping, because there's less pressure on their bladder. And when there's less pressure

fishermen — low pressure doesn't usually last long."

Low Means Slow

According to Woodward, fish are much more comfortable when there's stable high pressure, and tend to feed actively most anywhere within the water column. He also acknowledges the general cycles of high and low pressure and how fish react to them. "Let's say we're experiencing a prolonged period of high pressure and the fishing has been good. Then a cold front heads our way. Ahead of the front is low pressure. The fish can sense that the barometer is about to drop. So, right before the high begins to dissipate and the barometer falls, the fish respond with a change in feeding patterns. They'll often feed heavily right before the pressure drops. As it does, they become more uncomfortable and feed less aggressively. When the front passes and high pressure moves back in, the fish may not feed aggressively for at least 24 hours, since they're still adjusting.

"However, it's a different story a day or two after a high settles back in. The fish will have had time to stabilize and an intense bite can occur. When the pressure changes again, such as when another front moves in, the cycle repeats itself."

When the barometer sinks below 30 inches off his home coast of Georgia, Woodward doesn't bother fishing for big kings in less than 70 feet of water, even if the fishing had been good in previous days. Instead, he fishes farther offshore, in deeper water, where he believes the pressure change may be less pronounced and the kings less affected than those closer to shore. He also recognizes that the fish may be holding deeper in the water column during this period, and that he may have to experiment with the depth of his baits to score.

As Woodward mentioned, baitfish are also affected by barometric pressure. For example, falling pressure may force the bait to hold deeper and become less active, which would impact the fishing in the middle and upper levels of the water column

Bass by the Barometer
In New Jersey, Captain Terry Sullivan experiences similar behavior with striped bass. "There's nothing like it when we get inside that high-pressure bubble during the spring," says Sullivan. "That's when those brilliant, sunny days warm the bottom in the shallow backwaters. Usually on the third day of the high, the fish really turn on. These highs usually last three or four days before the weather changes."

Sullivan points out that one of his best nights of fishing came before an approaching front. With lightning flashing in the distance, the stripers turned on and aggressively struck the flies Sullivan and his charter clients were dead-drifting from their anchored boat.

"I've seen striped bass go on a wild feed right before the barometer began to drop," says Sullivan. "During summer, we get an upwelling effect ahead of a front. Right before our southeast wind shifts more southerly and begins

Knowledgeable anglers will adjust the depth and presentation of their baits to target species affected by pressure changes, such as this mutton snapper.

King mackerel often head to deeper water once a cold front arrives, and also tend to be less aggressive.

to blow, which precedes the front, it triggers a hot bite locally. The fish sense that a change in weather is about to occur and feed heavily right before the front. Once the wind goes hard south, they shut down. I guess they know they won't be eating for a few days, so they have to gorge themselves."

Offshore Affects

Barometric pressure affects things on the offshore grounds, too. I can recall a very slow day of dolphin trolling off South Florida one summer. As the afternoon progressed, a major thunderstorm began making its way off the land and threatening the offshore waters. With the storm still miles away, a light, cool breeze sprang up. About the time we decided to retrieve our baits and take off, a school of dolphin charged out from underneath what had been a totally dead weed line. We hung around just long enough to boat 15 fish before the storm forced our departure.

During the winter off South Florida, sailfish use cold fronts to aid their southerly migration. In this case, the arrival of high pressure after a cold front can spur incredible fishing, whereas low pressure seems to curb the activity. Ray Rosher, one of Miami's leading charter captains, shared his thoughts on how high and low pressure affect sailfish.

"A lot of people think it's all wind direction that gets the sailfish moving and feeding, but it's high pressure as well," says Rosher. "For example, you can have a light wind and rising pressure and the bite will be on. When high pressure moves in, we're in a cold front and the wind is from a northerly direction. When we have a strong northerly wind opposing the northbound Gulf Stream, the fish rise to the surface and use the wind direction and waves to help propel them against the Stream's current. Those are the conditions that really get them moving south. When they're tailing on the surface, they're burning more energy. And since they're more active, they must eat more. This is when those red-hot bites materialize.

"Low pressure is often accompanied by wind and waves from the south, which push north with the Gulf Stream. The southbound sailfish are now prone to more resistance at the surface. There are no northerly swells or winds for them to use to their advantage when swimming against the Stream. During this stage, I believe the fish stay deep to conserve energy. When this occurs, my flat and deep lines get the most bites.

"A good example occurred recently when my co-captain, Alex Castellanos, caught five sails in calm conditions. The next day, the barometric pressure increased and the wind shifted around from the north. Alex caught and released 15 out of 16 sailfish in less than four hours!"

As mentioned, there are numerous factors that influence fish behavior, and any one of them can make the difference between success and failure. The best strategy, of course, is to plan your fishing days around the peak conditions for your particular area and the local species. Unfortunately, that's a luxury few of us have, but now you can also blame the barometer if you come home empty-handed! ✳

Strips baits are excellent "pitch" baits, for a wide variety of game fish.

Chapter 15
The Right Pitch
Stand ready, and "pitch" for the win!

It was among the most humorous things I've seen on the water. Friend Harry Vernon III and I had a full spread of baits and teasers in play aboard my boat, as we trolled offshore of Boat Harbour in the Abacos. Off the transom, a 96-fish Strip-Teaser dredge created the illusion of a large bait ball some five feet beneath the surface. And this fake smorgasbord proved too much to overlook for a 40-pound bull dolphin. Lit up like a neon sign, the bull charged the dredge and tried to devour the reflective bait decals.

I swiftly grabbed the flat line outfit by that dredge, which towed a medium size ballyhoo at the surface and behind the dredge - and reeled the bait ahead of the feeding dolphin. But the dolphin was too focused on trying to eat fish decals to look upward at my bait.

I jigged the bait a few times, vying for its attention, to no avail. Suddenly, the dolphin turned passive and began losing its vibrant colors. Did we blow our opportunity to catch it?

What happened next really befuddled us; the dolphin, now a dull green and blue, slowly and lethargically swam into the middle of the dredge, and stayed there! Appearing quite relaxed, it seemed content to swim amongst the fish strips – and it did for a minute or so! Vernon later joked that it looked like the fish was either enjoying an invigorating massage from those plastic strips, or trying to breed with the fish dredge. Whatever its inspiration, we caught the dolphin, but it required the bait to be reeled well ahead of the commotion, and freespooled back – with the rod tip by the water - to where it drifted past the

dredge strips. When this happened, the dolphin lit up and consumed the gravely injured appearing bait! It was the perfect "pitch bait" tactic, executed with a flat line bait. We did have a designated conventional "pitch bait" outfit with a ballyhoo set aside for such an opportunity, but didn't need it in this case.

What's The Pitch?

Pitch baiting is primarily an offshore, big boat, billfishing tactic, where a minimum of a couple of outfits rigged with baits remain ready for instant deployment. Should a sailfish, white or blue marlin rise behind a surface teaser or dredge, an angler grabs the appropriate pitch bait outfit and "pitches" its bait back to the fish. If a fish is on a surface teaser, the angler's job is to position the bait so that it takes the

Just as one would rig an assortment of trolling baits to cover all sizes of game fish, keep at least two pitch offerings ready to go - a small bait for dolphin, white marlin and sailfish, and a large one for a blue marlin.

place of the teaser – which is being reeled up and away from the fish by the captain. The goal is to coax the fish off the teaser and onto the bait. Done correctly, the fish will hot and likely to feed aggressively. Combine this aggressiveness with the hook set being so close to the cockpit - which results in less line stretch, and successful hook-ups and "catches" are the norm.

When a fish rises behind a dredge, it's basically the same drill, though the dredge will remain in place. Like my earlier example with the dolphin, successfully hooking a fish in this situation often requires a bait to be freespooled back and down to just alongside or behind the dredge, where it appears as if the game fish has injured it. Should the tactic appear natural, the "charged up" fish will consume the bait, just as our big dolphin did.

Some may question the merits of pitch baiting, since a full spread of baits or lures are already in place. Won't they catch fish? A well-tuned trolling spread certainly catches fish, yet pitch baiting enables a crew to take advantage of one that rises onto teasers or behind dredges. And while Offshore Trolling 101 dictates positioning a bait near any teaser or dredge, there are instances when game fish will ignore these offerings. So, unless you have a pitch bait ready to go, you could miss what might be your one and only golden opportunity to catch that fish.

Many believe this tactic is strictly for large sportfishing vessels, with cockpit space for extra rods and well-honed teams to play out the pitch baiting game. This is a misconception, as small boat anglers can also incorporate pitch baiting into their arsenal, and run up their scores.

Successful Strategies

I've had the opportunity to fish with numerous big boat offshore pros, and many design their spreads and pitch baits around both large and small-to-medium size game fish. That is, they tend to fish large baits and teasers off one side of their vessel and small-to-medium baits and teasers off the other side. And they have at least two pitch bait outfits rigged for each situation.

For example, take one friend who spends spring and early summer marlin fishing in the Bahamas; he'll drag a large hookless teaser, with a rigged splashing mackerel positioned some ten feet behind that teaser, and from the short outrigger. The long outrigger on that side is often a horse ballyhoo. The pitch bait rods for that side include a Penn 70-International filled with 80-pound test monofilament, paired to a stand-up rod and small, fresh school dolphin. There's also a 50-pound class outfit that carries a splashing mackerel. In theory, that's the side where a blue marlin will likely rise, so these pitch baits stand ready for deployment here.

The opposite side often consists of a squid or cedar plug daisy chain and a mix of small, medium and large bally-hoo. Since this side should likely raise sailfish, white marlin and small blue marlin – along with dolphin, the designated pitch baits include a 50-pound class outfit with a large ballyhoo, and a small-to-medium ballyhoo paired with a small conventional outfit filled with 30-pound test monofilament.

This is not to imply that fish read magazines and, therefore, know which side of the bait spread to show, but rather that successful big game captains often design their "spreads" to attract specific fish, and then "back them up" with the appropriate pitch bait outfits. When a fish rises on a teaser, or even a bait – but doesn't strike, out goes a pitch bait. It's a thorough and aggressive way of fishing, and it creates positive results.

It must be noted that these individual pitch baits are rigged on appropriately sized hooks and leaders. That is, the blue marlin baits are on 300-pound test leaders and hooks with enough of a bite and strength to latch onto and hold these fish, whereas the smaller baits are on leaders varying from 130-pound test down to 80-pound test for the smallest ballyhoo. This way, should a small white, sail or dolphin come up, the light leader shouldn't interfere with the bait's action or the game fish consuming it. Try that with a larger bait and heavy leader, and the results will likely disappoint – hence the variation in bait and leader sizes and tackle.

Small Boats Too

Small boats are certainly not excluded from pitch baiting. Consider my troll-

Whenever using teasers and dredges, make sure to have "pitch" bait rods readily accessible.

ing efforts. When we're plying the offshore waters off South Florida and especially in the Bahamas, I'll often keep two pitch baits ready to go – one for large game, the other for light-tackle-sized game fish.

With these rods either in the mid-ship gunwales holders, or within the rocket launcher, their respective baits are placed in a bucket of cool sea water (we'll add a chunk of ice to the brine), within the live well, and sometimes even in the bait cooler itself. This way, the baits remain fresh and their rods

Big dolphin are willing "pitch" bait consumers.

and leaders out of the way. Yet, should a fish arise behind a teaser, they can be easily and quickly dispatched.

Exact pitch baits and tackle depend on where I'm fishing, and the likelihood of raising a large fish. However, the "large" pitch bait rod is generally a 50-pound class conventional outfit with a small to medium size splashing mackerel rigged onto 300-pound test fluorocarbon leader. Obviously, this bait is reserved for a blue marlin, and outsized dolphin.

The "lighter" pitch bait outfit carries a small to medium ballyhoo rigged onto either 80- or 130-pound fluorocarbon. And, as of late, that outfit is a large spinner. The spinning outfit offers the flexibility of casting at any fish you happen to see, as well as dropping back a bait. Plus, since the spinner is filled mostly with braided line and topped with a monofilament header, line capacity is not an issue; you can successfully bait sailfish, big dolphin and even tuna, without worrying over getting spooled.

Teaser Component

Teasers establish the foundation for pitch-baiting. The objective is to not only create more commotion and perceived panic/fear amongst the baits in the boat's wash, but to also draw fish close to the transom, where they can be pitched-baited. And if a fish refuses the pitch bait and begins dropping back, there are the close trolling baits and also the far- and center 'rigger baits that could entice a strike. So, in essence, you still have several possible shots at that fish, if you first lure it up close.

Using teasers can be as simple as cleating off a large hookless lure off each corner of the transom. Aboard my center console, I run a large Bost Americano teaser off the starboard side, and a Williamson squid spreader bar off the port side – both of which are controlled by T-Top-mounted teaser reels. I run the teaser lines through all three eyes of my Lee's 15-foot outriggers, to get these teasers working in the clean water well outside the prop wash. Incidentally, the drags on those teaser reels are set

to where they just hold them in place, yet not firm enough to where a fish crashing and running with a teaser can buckle an outrigger.

A pair of 96-fish Strip Teaser dredges ride from each transom cleat. Between the surface teasers and dredges, along with the flat lines and short outrigger baits, there is a lot of commotion stirring behind the boat. In short, a good recipe for raising fish into pitch baiting range.

Think Variety

As mentioned earlier, pitch-baiting is primarily a billfishing tactic, but it certainly isn't limited to them. I've used the method to score plenty of dolphin, and – occasionally – for casting small ballyhoo and baits into busting fish, like blackfins, skipjacks and even yellowfins.

There's no denying its effectiveness. I know. I've caught fish doing it while traveling and fishing aboard big boats, and even aboard my own center console. If you're looking to ramp up your trolling game, this is - without a doubt - an excellent tactic to incorporate, ASAP! ✳

Top shots are ideal for gaining line capacity, for when pursuing large game fish, like this blue marlin, on both spin- and conventional tackle.

Chapter 16
The Top-Shot Revolution
Rethinking the line-reel relationship...

It might appear a bit unusual to chunk for sizable yellowfin tuna with 12- and 16-pound-class conventional tackle unless you're simply seeking a prolonged fight on light line for bragging rights. After all, who would compromise delicious yellowfin tuna steaks by burning out a tuna or risk such a quality fish to sharks via a long, tedious battle? In tuna fishing, the quicker you bring the fish to gaff, the better. Yet numerous anglers are indeed bringing such light tackle to the game - save for one major modification: heavy line.

Confused? Don't be. Welcome to the top-shot revolution, in which ever-increasing droves of anglers are going the braid-monofilament top-shot route to gain line capacity, and also comfort, when pursuing their favorite big game fish. The quality build of modern reels and the effectiveness of their drags make heavy lines manageable on smaller reels; the strength versus diameter of braided lines allows more heavier-test line to be loaded on the smaller-capacity reels. It's this match that has opened the door to the top-shot revolution. And you can sift me into that group, as I've converted my 16-pound-class lever-drag reels to this setup for my Bahamas yellowfin tuna chunking. I've also switched over many of my lighter reef, offshore, live-bating and casting outfits - spinners included. More on these outfits later.

The Conversion
I became a big convert a few seasons ago, when a couple of friends in the Northeast showed me how they spool a Penn 16 with 80-pound braided line followed by a 200-yard top shot of 50-pound-test monofilament line. This has become a hot setup for canyon tuna chunking.

The advantage of this, compared to bigger and heavier 50-pound and larger tackle, is it enables anglers to hook, fight and land one tuna after another with very little fatigue. Plus, some charter captains have found the lighter reels prove much easier for inexperienced clients to handle through the full process of chunking, hooking a fish, removing the outfit from its gunwale holder and then fighting the fish. This makes such folks who pay just shy of a king's ransom for an overnight canyon charter feel like an essential and effective part of the team and not simply spectators.

Step One
Fill between 1/2- and 3/4- of the reel spool with braided line.

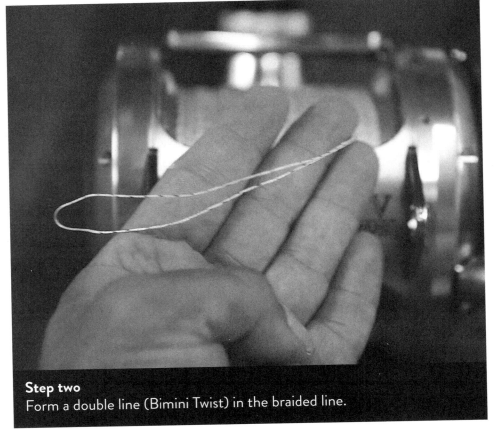

Step two
Form a double line (Bimini Twist) in the braided line.

Bahamas and south Florida. Naturally, the same would hold true for the Gulf of Mexico, Southern California and Mexico's Baja California.

What You Gain

The exact amount of line capacity acquired is based on the ratio of braided line to monofilament line you opt for - and yes, there are preferences, based on species and conditions. However, as a general rule, you should come close to or exceed the amount of line a specific reel is rated to carry. For example, my Penn 16 International is advertised as holding 480 yards of 30-pound-test monofilament line (a common choice of line for this reel, which holds an exorbitant 1,075 yards of straight 16-pound-test monofilament) or 700 yards of 80-pound-test braided line. For my Bahamas tuna chunking, my reels are spooled with approximately 400 yards of 80-pound-test Sufix Performance Braid followed by a 200-yard top shot of 50-pound-test Sufix Superior monofilament line, for a total of around 600 yards of heavy line - very impressive considering the small and light stature of these reels. Of course, line capacity can be bumped up proportionately by using more braid than mono.

This setup gives not only more-than-ample line capacity to whip the larger yellowfins but also the option to deploy these outfits on the troll for a variety of species; should we hook a marlin, there's enough line for us to chase down, fight and beat the fish. Again, like with the canyons example mentioned earlier, I'm seeking the comfort and ease these lighter outfits bring when chunking and live-bating

Another huge advantage, naturally, is line capacity: Should a large tuna or swordfish pick off a bait behind an anchored boat, this setup should provide enough line capacity for fighting the fish while it remains on the hook or, at the very least, allow ample time for tossing the anchor line and float ball and chasing it down. So I reasoned that if such a setup works wonders in the mid-Atlantic and Northeast canyons, it should prove ideal for my offshore pursuits in the tuna, along with the strength the braid-mono top shot provides.

Trolling Formulas

Even my 30-, 50- and 70-pound-class dedicated trolling outfits adhere to the same braid-mono top-shot ratios. That is, 50-pound-test braid backs 30-pound monofilament, 80-pound-test braid is behind 50-pound-test monofilament, and 100-pound-test braid is behind 80-pound-test monofilament for these reel classes, respectively. In this case, I'm seeking extra line capacity, especially when I'm in the far southeastern Bahamas, where hooking a large wahoo, marlin or tuna is likely.

Since braided line has a significantly smaller diameter than nylon monofilament of the same breaking strength, I opt for a stronger braid backing than the designated line class for the reel. I adhere to the latter when choosing the monofilament top shot. One exception is my tuna-chunking outfit, which uses the 80-50 ratio. But that's for specialized fishing.

General Logic

I'm often asked why I don't use braided line exclusively, along with a long monofilament or fluorocarbon leader, for offshore trolling. When trolling offshore, I like the inherent stretch in monofilament line, which acts as a cushion. This comes into play with marlin and other powerful and perhaps acrobatic fish, which surge and run and may leap quickly and powerfully. This extra bit of stretch can be just enough to keep the hook from tearing free or straightening out. Also, the monofilament is much more forgiving when multiple tunas or other

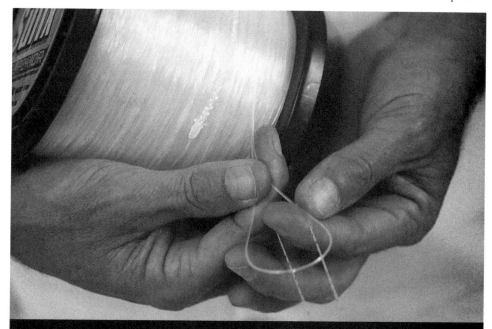

Step Three
Form a double line (Bimini Twist) in the spool of monofilament, and then lay the "loops" of both the monofilament and braided line on top of each other.

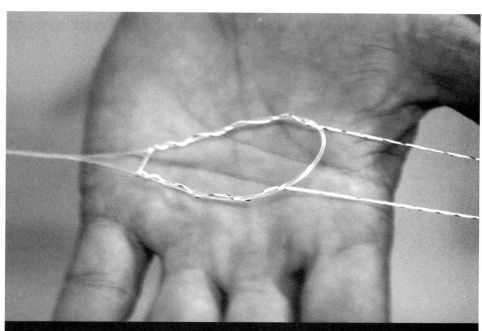

Step Four
Begin the Cat's Paw connection by passing the spool of line several times through both the monofilament and braided line "loops".

doubleheaders create crossed lines. Braided lines in such a predicament often result in cutoffs.

Many people attach braid to monofilament with small offshore swivels, which provide a quick connection. I've never felt comfortable hearing and

feeling these swivels pass through the rod guides when I've used such setups. They've always held, but I worry about the wear on the guides and the possibility of their corroding and failing if not properly cared for.

When joining braid to mono, I

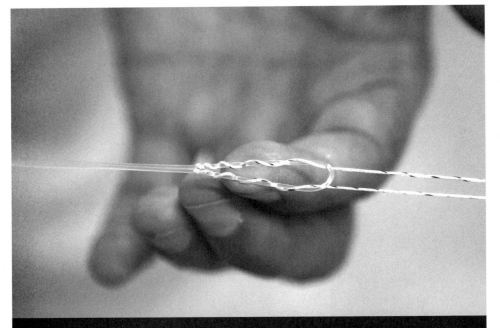

Step Five
Gradually pull on the monofilament and braided lines and snug down the Cat's Paw knot.

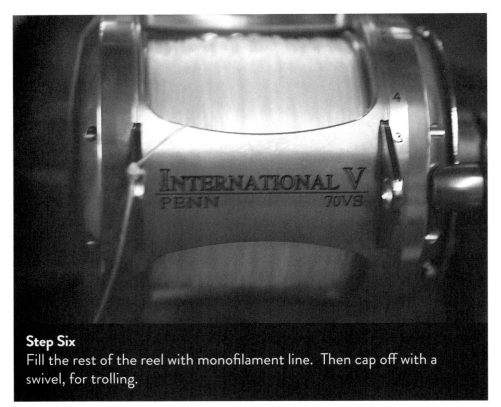

Step Six
Fill the rest of the reel with monofilament line. Then cap off with a swivel, for trolling.

prefer the cat's-paw connection. This entails putting a short double line in the braid and a short double line in the mono (keep the mono on the spool during this stage). Then interlock the two loops, and pass the spool of monofilament through these loops five times. Snug down the connection, and wind on the monofilament top shot. The connection is small and secure.

Smaller Stuff Too!

As previously mentioned, I've even gone the braid-mono route for my smaller nearshore and offshore tackle. For example, looking for line capacity and solid abrasion-resistance when anchored up and free-lining live baits on a reef, I've spooled my small and next largest conventional reels primarily with 30- and 50-pound braided line, respectively, and a 20-foot 30-pound-test fluorocarbon top shot. This way we can hook an outsize king mackerel - and when we're not fast enough to reel away a bait, the occasional shark - on the sporty small reels and not have to get off the anchor to pursue them. We often use these same reels when drifting the reefs for a mixed bag that includes everything from sailfish to grouper to cobia. On the drift, line capacity isn't as critical an issue, but it sure is nice having enough backbone to battle fish on such small outfits.

As for spinning tackle, this has become a go-to setup for those big offshore spinning reels. In fact, I've even spooled my smaller 12- and 20-pound-class spinners with 20- and 30-pound-test braided line and 12- and 20-pound-test mono top shots, respectively. These top shots average around 20 feet in length. Again, I'm looking for line capacity with the braid and enough cushion to absorb surges with the mono. These top shots, incidentally, are not the actual leaders, except when we're casting to blackfin tuna. These spinners come into play when casting lures and baits to dolphin, cobia and blackfin tuna.

In the offshore world, the braid-mono top shot is a hot setup for the reasons outlined here. It brings a certain comfort to fishing, with tackle that's strong enough to whip powerful fish yet light enough not to wear out the angler. Best of all, it puts big fish in the boat and even bigger grins on everyone's faces. And what's not to like about that? ❋

The Quick Change Ballyhoo - it's deadly and always stays in the game!

Chapter 17
Quick-Change Ballyhoo
Proven rigging tricks keep your baits in the water when the bite is on

Capt. John Oughton absolutely terrorizes the bluefin, yellowfin and bigeye tuna when they migrate anywhere near his home port of Ocean City, Maryland. At the helm of his 50-foot Evans, *That's Right*, Oughton runs wherever and however long it takes to get on the fish. He's no slacker. And when he's in the action, he and mate Jason Genther strive to be as proficient as possible at catching them.

One key to the team's success is the quick-change ballyhoo rig they use trolling for tuna. Rather than

meticulously rigging several dozen baits in advance and layering them on trays in a cooler, Oughton and Genther rely on their quick-change rigs to keep from missing a beat - or a fish. This rig consists of a leader (usually 100- or 130-pound-test fluorocarbon) and a hook (based on the size of the ballyhoo), with a sinker (usually ¼ ounce to 1½ ounces) riding on the leader just in front of the loop to which the hook is attached. They favor weighted skirts ahead of their baits. From there, things become a little different.

'Hoo Fooler
Because wahoo are always possible, Oughton uses a few inches of No.10 single-strand wire to form a loop alongside that of the fluorocarbon leader that connects the hook. One strand of the wire, along with the fluorocarbon, goes through the hook eye, and both strands of the wire follow the fluorocarbon through two 1.6 mm sleeves that, when crimped, complete the connection. The goal is for the wire-reinforced loop to prevent wahoo from severing the fluorocarbon leader, providing the fish doesn't hit well

Quick-Change Ballyhoo

This variation on the conventional ballyhoo pin rig takes only seconds to put together but provides a secure connection between bait and leader. Here's how to do it.

1: Lay the rig and ballyhoo side by side, and visualize where the hook point will exit the bait.

2: Slip the hook inside the ballyhoo's throat latch, and thread it through the bait. Poke the point of the hook out the bait's belly.

above the hook. The other purpose of the wire is to form the pin that rides at a 90-degree angle to the leader, which is run underneath and through both jaws of the ballyhoo to help secure the bait to the rig.

In place of a length of Monel or soft copper wire to secure the bait, Oughton utilizes a No. 32 rubber band affixed to the loop of the leader that holds the hook. This is where the quick-change feature comes into play: Both Oughton and Genther claim they can change out a ballyhoo within seconds by unwrapping the rubber band, removing the damaged bait and, with the same rubber band, rigging a fresh bait to the hook. With practice, this can be accomplished in less time than it takes to get into the cooler, select a ballyhoo, uncoil the leader and change out the damaged rig.

Several of these basic rigs are fabricated in advance with various

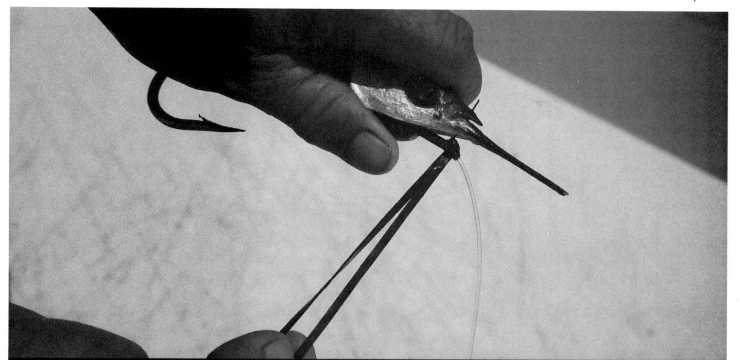

3: Line up the wire pin directly underneath the bait's lower jaw, then push it through both the lower and the upper jaws.

4: Wrap the rubber band tightly behind the pin twice, and follow with two wraps ahead of the pin. Repeat until you come to the very end of the rubber band.

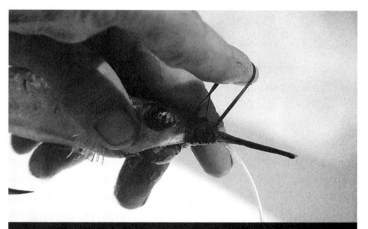

5: Stretch the rubber-band end loop over the upright pin. When this is done correctly, the rubber band will snug down over the pin, keep the jaws of the bait closed and secure the bait to the rig.

sizes of hooks and, sometimes, leader strengths. "This gives us the latitude of choosing which size ballyhoo to put in the spread," says Oughton. "We have a tray in a cooler with different sizes of un-rigged ballyhoo. We can grab the size we want, secure it to the rig and get it back out behind the boat in no time at all."

Oughton says this particular rig goes into play when the tuna are

around and the trolling speed's averaging around 5 or 6 knots. "If we do more conventional trolling at higher speeds," he says, "we'll go with the typical ballyhoo rigs with Monel or soft copper wire, since they handle the trolling stresses much better. But for slower trolling when we are on the fish and not searching for them, this rig is tough to top."

Recipe for Speed

Mate Genther layers the unrigged ballyhoo in a cooler. Some of the baits have the eyes removed (to prevent them from filling with water and bugging) and have been milked of their stomach contents, whereas others remain unprepped. Only after a ballyhoo has been affixed to the rig does Genther crush the backbone, to limber

6: Before placing the bait in the spread, crush the backbone for additional flexibility and swimming action and snap off the beak.

To replace a bait, simply undo the rubber band, remove the damaged bait and affix a fresh one.

it up, and snap off the beak. The crushing is done with an index finger and thumb by squeezing gently yet firmly along the bait's lateral line. Done correctly, you can hear the slight crunching sound as the backbone compresses.

On the way to the grounds, Genther attaches the prepped baits to their rigs and then dispatches them when the trolling begins. Gunning for bluefins, Genther and Oughton deploy eight baits; for yellowfins, they set 14 baits in the spread. When a bait gets hit and the fish is boated, Genther removes the hook, undoes the rubber band, removes what's left of the bait, puts on a fresh ballyhoo, secures it with the same rubber band and gets that bait back in position within seconds. He'll change out a leader only if it has been chafed or nicked.

The effectiveness of the quick-change rig really comes into play when multiple tunas are hooked or when there's one bite right after another. In system-like fashion, a fish is boated, the hook removed, and the rig rebaited and then redeployed within moments, keeping nearly all the baits fishing during a hot bite. I had the opportunity to spend some time fishing with Oughton and Genther and watched this rig in play. It's fast and effective and keeps bait soak time to a maximum. And best of all, it catches fish! ✳

Water surface temperature breaks serve as mini-ecosystems that support everything from phytoplankton to big game pelagics.

Chapter 18
Temperature Rules
Follow the water temperature and your offshore score will soar

In offshore fishing, water temperature can be everything. Success often boils down to finding a significant "thermal break" or "convergence zone" along a major current or its offshoots, such as eddies or fingers. These breaks are usually formed when warm, offshore water collides with cooler inshore water. Where the two water masses meet, a temperature boundary forms.

Significant convergence zones — usually marked by a dramatic fluctuation in water temperature and an abrupt change in water color — often foster massive plankton blooms, which become the foundation for mini ecosystems that eventually attract large predators. Find the food (i.e., bait) along these breaks and you'll likely find the game fish.

Locating convergence zones and

temperature breaks is especially important in the Northeast. Given that the Gulf Stream can be well over 100 miles offshore in some areas, many anglers rely on offshoots of the Stream, called eddies, to bring tropical water and the game fish associated with it within range. Warm-water eddies are circulating masses that have broken off from the Gulf Stream, and spin in a clockwise direction as they head inshore. When such an eddy moves onto the continental shelf, fishermen have a much shorter run to the fish.

Crucial Knowledge

"Knowing the whereabouts of the temperature boundaries is absolutely critical," says Captain Terry Stansel, who skippers the 54-foot Hatteras, *Hatterascal*, and participates in some

20 tournaments each year. "In the Mid-Atlantic and Northeast, we're traveling from one tournament to the next, and rarely have the luxury of pre-fishing an area. Surface-temperature charts and ocean-circulation analyses give us a good indication as to where we want to look for fish, rather than merely running offshore and hoping for the best. They take the guesswork out of the game.

"My surface-temperature gauge becomes more important than my GPS when I'm getting close to an area. Off the Mid-Atlantic, finding a three-degree temperature break with greenish-blue water on one side and royal-blue water boiling on the other side is the ultimate. Just last season, off Ocean City, Maryland, there were a whole bunch of these rips offshore, with three or four boats working each

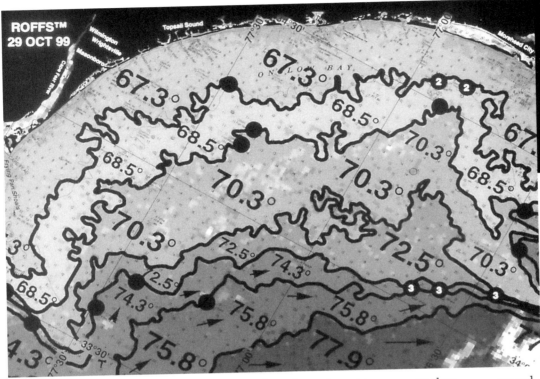

ROFFS™
29 OCT 99

Fishing forecast analyses, such as those offered by Roffer's, includes the location of significant water temperature breaks and the ones that most likely hold bait and game fish.

rip. The white marlin were on the rips, and it seemed like all the boats were hooking up. It was like Venezuela!"

of Mexico, where big-game anglers monitor the Loop Current and the whereabouts of any eddies or fila-

crowd. David Brackmann of the Caliente fleet, based in California and Cabo San Lucas, claims that he and his

> When I'm trolling for dolphin off South Florida, for instance, I often consult a surface-temperature chart to find the precise edge of the Gulf Stream, which changes over time.

While large East Coast eddies occur almost exclusively north of Cape Hatteras, Gulf Stream spin-offs around the Carolinas flow counter-clockwise, which is distinctive of cold-core eddies. As in the Northeast, these eddies and their accompanying temperature breaks have the potential to establish nutrient- and plankton-rich zones closer to shore, where anglers can find tuna, dolphin, wahoo and marlin.

It's really no different in the Gulf

ments that have broken away from it. When these bluewater features move close to shore and "park" over prime bottom structure, such as canyons, ridges and the 100-fathom curve, they set up potentially productive zones that are within reach of large and mid-sized boats.

West Coast Currents
Off Southern California and Baja, locating the right water temperature is just as important to the offshore

skippers live by these breaks. "When the albacore move in, we look for the biggest temperature break we can find," he says. "A two-degree break over a distance of a mile or two is very significant.

"I get my [surface-temperature] information from Terrafin. They send me a daily report, which I print out on a color printer. Before I go fishing, I lay out a week's worth of reports and study the movement of the water. I'll determine which significant break or

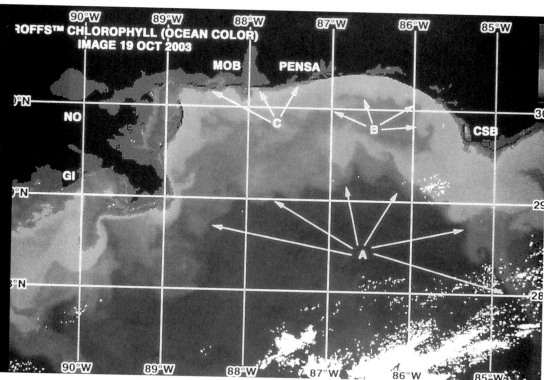

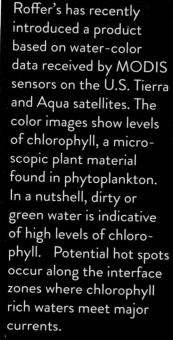

Roffer's has recently introduced a product based on water-color data received by MODIS sensors on the U.S. Tierra and Aqua satellites. The color images show levels of chlorophyll, a microscopic plant material found in phytoplankton. In a nutshell, dirty or green water is indicative of high levels of chlorophyll. Potential hot spots occur along the interface zones where chlorophyll rich waters meet major currents.

eddy is sitting the longest in one spot, and which area looks the most promising. And that's where we'll head.

"Our California current brings cold water down to Mexico, while a warm-water current flows north from Mexico. During summer, the California current weakens and enables the warm-water current to move closer to shore. When that happens, it tends to bring some of the tropical fish with it.

"It pays to know the whereabouts of the current edges. Down off Baja the last few years, we've had some cold water coming from California. Because of this, we've been finding the better thermal breaks up in the Sea of Cortez, which holds the warmer water. We'll take yellowfins on the warmer edges and striped marlin on the cold side of the breaks."

While thermal breaks are unde-

niably important in areas where the major current is far from shore, they can be just as beneficial off southern Florida and the Bahamas, where deep water and the Gulf Stream are very close. Along Florida's southeast coast, offshoots from the Gulf Stream form elongated "fingers" that curve away from the main current. The more significant ones, which are often highlighted by stronger current, will produce fish.

Bait on the Edge
While productive fishing is possible along any major break, another key ingredient is bait. If you happen upon a major thermal or color edge and there are no signs of bait on the surface or on the sounder, it's often best to keep looking. Look for bait along other portions of the same break (if fishing an

eddy), or inshore or offshore of that zone. Once you find the bait concentrations, stick it out and keep a close eye on your depthsounder. If the fish aren't already on the feed, they should be sooner or later.

Major currents or eddies that flow over pronounced bottom structure, such as canyons, seamounts and sharply sloping bottom, harbor even more potential, especially if they remain stationary for an extended period of time. A strong current that flows over structure creates upwellings of nutrients that feed plankton blooms. In addition, baitfish become displaced from the deep structure and attracted to the food chain being established by the plankton. The longer the temperature boundary remains in one place, the more concentrated the bait and game fish become. That's why station-

Anglers pursuing highly migratory offshore species, like this bluefin tuna, rely on water temperature charts and analyses to narrow their search.

ary eddies are so treasured by knowledgeable fishermen.

As mentioned, temperature breaks can be very important off South Florida and the Bahamas. Compared to the sometimes large temperature variations found off the Northeast and Mid-Atlantic, a one- or two-degree temperature break is considered significant.

When I'm trolling for dolphin off South Florida, for instance, I often consult a surface-temperature chart to find the precise edge of the Gulf Stream, which changes over time. One day the Stream's western edge might be eight miles off Port Everglades Inlet, while the next day it might be 12 miles offshore. I try to establish the whereabouts of the Stream's western edge in relation to my home inlet. If the edge happens to be out around the continental shelf drop-off in 600 feet of water, I'll have the advan-

tage of fishing a stronger current edge that creates a plankton- and bait-rich zone, as well as any weed lines or flotsam that may collect there. In addition, I'll be fishing over a pronounced bottom contour, which the fish follow during their migrations.

Getting the Info

There are many services that provide information on the whereabouts of major surface-temperature breaks and water movement. Subscribers generally receive a detailed chart via fax, e-mail or off a website showing the location of various surface-temperature zones. Some services even provide an analysis of the information and pinpoint areas that offer the best chance of holding fish.

However, it's important to keep in mind that a particular eddy, convergence

zone or the main current itself could have shifted by the time you leave the dock. Therefore, it's important to watch for rips, bait and color changes, and pay strict attention to the temperature gauge and depthsounder as you approach your intended target. You may find what you were looking for miles ahead of or beyond the location indicated on the temperature chart.

Considering the price of an offshore boat, let alone what it costs to operate it for a day of fishing, a water-temperature analyses is a bargain. For an extra $30 to $65 dollars per trip you can eliminate much of the guesswork as to where the fish may be. And when you have to run many miles offshore and back, that money will come back to you in terms of fuel savings, not to mention bragging rights at the dock. ✳

Line markers are a very important part of shark fishing, as they help anglers set baits at precise depths, and score more fish - like this New Jersey Mako.

Chapter 19
Tying the Perfect Line Marker
An expert's tips on this useful offshore skill

Hard-core offshore anglers often utilize loops on their fishing lines. These loops aren't the result of lines that were badly twisted by trolling without swivels, but rather they are waxed-thread markers and attachment points positioned securely to fishing lines at precise intervals.

These loops may be attached to outrigger clips to ensure trolling baits and lures ride at specific distances behind the boat, or they may secure weights or lights to fishing lines, such as when drifting for swordfish, sharks

or tuna. Streamlined loopless markers serve as visual indicators as to how many feet or yards of line are off the reel and lend the precision required when wire-line trolling for wahoo and grouper, and even drifting for big game fish. Both looped and loopless markers play an instrumental role in offshore fishing.

Harry Vernon III likes to get looped when he's fishing, figuratively. A proprietor of Capt. Harry's Fishing Supply in Miami, Vernon uses loops to attach his fishing lines to outrigger clips, as well as weights and lights to

his swordfish tackle. Nicknamed the Wire-Line Wizard, Vernon also uses loopless markers at 50- and 100-foot increments on his wire outfits so, whether he's pulling fast for wahoo or moderately for grouper, he knows exactly how much wire line is in the water. This helps him compute just how deep the lure is riding given the weight and amount of wire line in the water, the weight of the lure and the speed of the boat. He's deadly precise and has the catches to prove it. In fact, he's fresh off a victory in a Bahamas winter wahoo tournament.

LOOP MARKER

Step 1
Tie the waxed thread to the fishing line with an overhand knot.

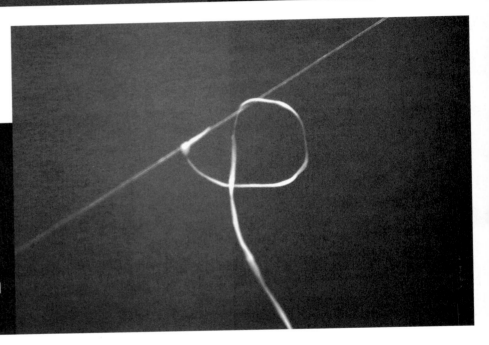

Step 2
Add a half hitch above the overhand knot. It is important to keep tension on the fishing line and to securely snug down the half hitch to prevent it from slipping. It is also important that the second half hitch is cinched tightly over the tag end of the initial half hitch on the line to provide a solid bite and a better holding foundation.

Step 3
Add another 15 to 20 half hitches. Make the final half hitch, but don't cinch it. Instead, adjust the hitch to form the desired size of loop and then tie two half hitches on the line to establish the loop size.

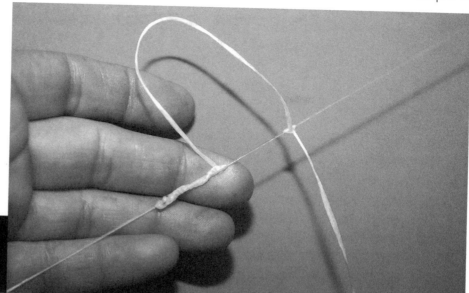

Step 4
On the outside of the loop, continue with 15 to 20 more half hitches.

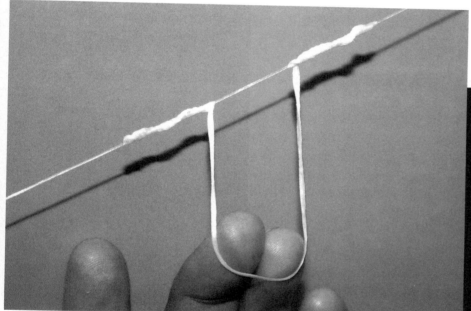

Step 5
Complete the construction with a reverse half hitch wrapped around the fishing line six times before you pull it tight. Pull tag until it cinches down over itself just inside the end of the marker. This will prevent the connection from unraveling in the water or when running through the rod guides. Trim the tag end as close to the knot as possible.

Marking lines is very important when fishing for swordfish, particularly when day-dropping for them.

LOOPLESS MARKER

Repeat all but Step 3 for a more streamlined, loop-free marker.

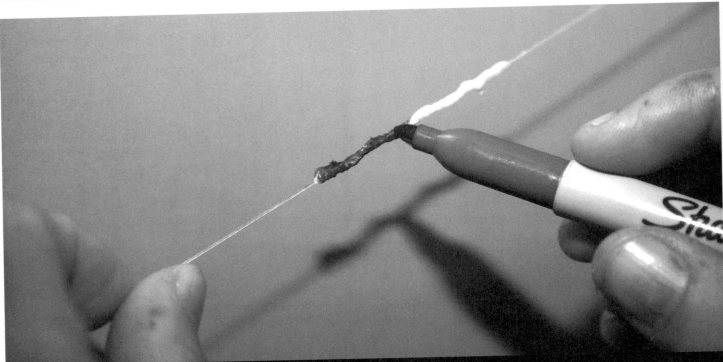

Use permanent markers to color-code the individual line markers. For example, color the initial marker blue and the next red, followed by black, orange, etc. This will enable you to quickly determine if you have 100, 200, 300 or 400 feet of line out (if you've measured in 100-foot increments). Go beyond that, and you can use two colors per marker - for example, red and blue, orange and black.

For wahoo, after the initial 100-foot marker, Vernon marks his wire line in 50-foot increments. In addition to color-coding them, he ties a 2-inch marker every 100 feet and a 1-inch marker at every 50 feet. This arrangement provides color and size to help him quickly determine the amount of line in the water.

Drift anchors continue to help score more and bigger king mackerel, by allowing live baits maximum time to thoroughly "soak" over quality bottom structure.

Chapter 20
Using Drift Anchors
Drift anchors help you catch more fish

Catching fish is a continuous game of fine-tuning. And when drifting, one vital piece of equipment is a drift anchor, or drift sock, which helps fine-tune the speed at which a boat drifts over an expanse of promising structure, a wreck or even schooling fish.

When setting out a spread of live baits from my 28-foot center console in pursuit of sailfish and kingfish, I'll generally start my drift without the drift anchor. My speed over ground is quicker, drifting sockless, so we cover more ground and better our odds of finding fish. Once we strike fish, we put the drift anchor out and can stay on top of them much longer.

However, if we're faced with a swift drift due to a fast current or moderate breeze, the drift anchor goes out regardless, even if fish are scattered. That's because a fast drift hinders the placement and action of live baits, bottom baits and even jigs. Without a drift anchor, additional weight may be required to keep baits in specific positions within the water column. And

excess weight could be sensed by a fish picking up a bait and also reduce our ability to visually monitor rod tips for subtle pickups. Furthermore, it's more difficult for smaller, less-durable baits - like pilchards and ballyhoo - to weather the rigors of quick drifts than it is for heartier, stronger baits like blue runners, goggle-eyes and tinker mackerel. When jigging or bottomfishing on the drift, constant free-spooling is a must to reach and hold near bottom; if the boat drifts too quickly, it leaves the lines too far behind to be effective.

Whenever there's a fast current or wind drift, deploy a drift anchor, slow the boat's drift rate, and thoroughly fish your zones. You'll catch more fish, versus blowing right over prime fish habitat.

WIND

Depth Marker

10-ft. Leader

Sea Anchor

Though we use a drift anchor mainly for our offshore pursuits, it is by no means reserved strictly for reefs and blue water. We've used it on windy days over shallow patch reefs for mackerel, snappers and groupers, and even over some of the deeper grass beds in Florida's Biscayne Bay for seatrout.

Purpose Built

There is a significant difference between a sea anchor and a drift anchor, though they appear to do the same thing in their basic forms. A sea anchor is a safety device first and foremost, one which must be approved by the U.S. Coast Guard. Since its main purpose is to save lives by keeping the bow into the seas when a boat becomes disabled in water that is too deep to anchor in, it's built to exacting stand-ards. Failure is not an option.

Furthermore, a sea anchor is usually several times larger than a drift anchor for the same-size vessel. When choosing a sea anchor, the general rule is to select one with a diameter that's double the draft of the boat for mono-hulls. That is, a boat with a draft of 3 feet would require a sea anchor with a

Sea- and drift anchors are a must when kite fishing for sailfish and kingfish, as they slow the boat's rate of speed and keep the baits working longer in a productive zone.

6-foot diameter. The anchor's maximum pull (strength) in tons should equal its diameter in feet. So a 6-foot sea anchor should be able to withstand a pull of six tons. Then, to ensure the sea anchor works properly, the amount of nylon rode paid out should be the result of doubling the wave height and then multiplying by 10. This means that in a 6-foot sea, for example, you'd need to pay out 120 feet of rode (6 x 2 x 10). With Dacron and polyester rodes, double the wave height and multiply by 20 (nylon has about 10 percent stretch, Dacron and polyester roughly 5 percent). Failure to use the proper length of rode could cause the line to snap or destroy the sea anchor. A drift anchor, by comparison, is a specialized tool for particular types of fishing when you need to slow the drift of the boat. Although it could keep the bow into the seas, it is not built to the exacting standards of a sea anchor and, therefore, should not be considered a worthy substitute. A drift anchor uses its funnel shape to catch water and restrict flow through the small opening at its opposite end. This generates drag and slows a boat's drift. While a sea anchor requires an exorbitant amount of rode, a drift anchor needs only enough rode so it rises and falls in sync with the boat. If the rode is too short, the bow of the boat could dip down as the anchor rises on the crest, and vice versa. Should that occur, the anchor could repeatedly collapse and fill, which can stress and possibly break the chute or rode.

Components

The components of a drift anchor include its conical chute, rode, swivel shackle, shackle to join the rode to the anchor, and trip line, which floats (if it's made from polypropylene) or has a float attached to it so that it remains separated from the main rode and within easy reach. The trip line allows the angler to collapse the chute and pull it into the boat to fight a fish by the boat or move to another spot.

There are several brands of drift anchors catering to various fishing styles and budgets. The Drift Control drift sock (www.lindyfishingtackle. com) is a popular choice catering to inshore, nearshore and some offshore fishermen. The company's top-selling Original series is available in four sizes, ranging from approximately 25 inches to 5 feet, and costs from $55 to $85. The socks are fabricated from lightweight nylon and fortified with 1-inch nylon straps. Their upper cylinder floats, and bottom weights promote swift openings and limited rotation. They're popular with bay and nearshore coastal anglers drifting for halibut, fluke, striped bass, seatrout, redfish and mackerel.

When drifting a weedline or rip and chunking or live-baiting for dolphin, try deploying a drift anchor. In addition to slowing forward motion, the drift anchor may also attract dolphin to it.

For midsize and large fishing boats that frequent rougher waters, Wave Tamer drift socks (www.lindyfishingtackle.com) are a bit more durable and less prone to spinning, sinking or collapsing in such conditions. A spring-biased opening and top flotation promote quick deployment and retrieval. They range from 3 to 14 feet and cost from $70 to $185.

The Hercules of Drift Anchors

A popular choice among many serious offshore anglers is the Para-Tech sea anchor line (www.seaanchor.com). These are more in line with true sea anchors yet are widely used for fishing from big center consoles and midsize and large offshore fishing boats. They can be found assisting the drifts of many crafts fishing for tuna, swordfish, shark and sailfish, from the Northeast canyons to

Even fluke anglers can benefit by remaining longer over prime structure, via a drift anchor.

the Pacific. Their performance and durability - particularly in rough seas - make them a hit among the offshore crowd. In addition, they do double duty as a safety device should a boat become disabled in rough seas.

Para-Tech has eight models, ranging from 6 to 40 feet and priced from $270 to $4,200, including a deployable stowage bag, heavy-duty shackle, float line and instruction manual, but not the floats, anchor rode or swivel shackle.

Harry Vernon III, an ardent live-bait sailfish and swordfish angler from Miami and owner of Capt. Harry's Fishing Supply, swears by his 15-foot Para-Tech sea anchor. "It's the best there is," says Vernon. "It keeps my 31-foot center console's bow into the sea and helps stabilize it. No matter how rough the water, we can comfortably fish a full spread of baits behind the boat. I chose the 15-footer because I want my boat to nearly sit still. It really cuts down on drift speed, and I stay over good bottom much longer."

The manufacturers of drift anchors have charts to help you determine the most effective one for your size of boat. Keep in mind that you can fine-tune the drift with the size of anchor you select.

Drift anchors are indeed a drag - but in a good way. Every inshore, nearshore and offshore boat that drift-fishes even occasionally should have one. Find one angler who wouldn't want to stay longer on top of a feeding school of fish, and I'll show you a person who has no business being out there in the first place.

Where Drift Anchors Shine

Deep-Jigging: Slows the vessel's drift so that deep jigs and flutter-style jigs can easily reach bottom and be worked effectively. Allows an angler to go with a lighter jig to get the job done, especially when braided line is used.

Bottomfishing With Natural Bait: Reduces drift speed so sinkers and baits remain on the bottom longer.

Lighter weights can be used under a slow drift.

Stealthy Approaches: For quietly drifting into schooling or feeding fish in shallow water. Get upwind, deploy the drift anchor and unobtrusively "slide" into the fish.

Competing With Other Boats: When the noise and ruckus of boats working over a school of fish sends them down or slows the bite, try drifting through the fish quietly and without power.

Wreck Fishing: Deploying a drift anchor enables you to position an attractive spread of live baits throughout the water column and keep them in the strike zone over that wreck much longer.

Shark, Tuna, Sailfish & Swordfish: A must-have item when drifting in the canyons, over deep peaks and depressions in the Gulf Stream, over reefs and along color changes. ❊

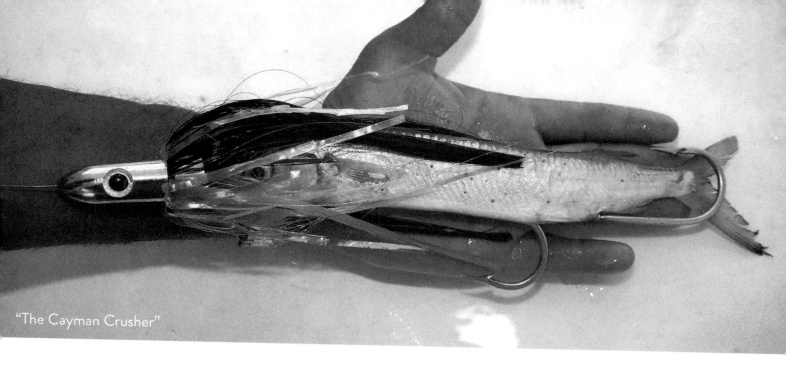

"The Cayman Crusher"

Chapter 21
The Cayman Crusher
The trolling rig wahoo fear!

To say it had been a "phenome-
nally amazing" morning would
still fall way short of describ-
ing the "bite" we experienced off the
Cayman Islands this past November.
Within a two hour window, between
sunup and 8:00 a.m., we boated 10
wahoo to 57-pounds, two yellowfin
tuna to 45-pounds and released a blue
marlin. By noon, our wahoo total increased to 15, and we even scored two
more yellowfins and a dolphin. We
could have caught even more, for sure,
but with plenty of fish iced down for
the entire crew, we called it a day!

I was shooting an episode for my
televisions series in the Caymans, with
friend and noted marine artist – Carey
Chen. We were aboard the 65-foot
Hatteras "Cayman Time", captained
by Chris Briggs and Eric Rivers and
with Jacob McTaggert, Nick Jones and
Charles Ebanks working the cockpit.
This was a virtual "dream team" of
some of the best anglers on Grand
Cayman, and the action was taking

place off Pickle Bank, some 80 miles
from Grand Cayman.

What I found equally amazing
was that we lost very few wahoo, our
intended target. We missed a few fish,
but when the smoke cleared, I'd say we
enjoyed at least a 95-percent success rate
on hooking and holding onto the striped
speedsters. Furthermore, it was a
chore removing hooks from the fish we
boated, illustrating just how efficient our
trolling rigs were. Compared to some
of the "sleek" and "racy" wahoo lures
on the market, our baits would appear
as "simple" and "basic"; they were all
Ilander-skirted ballyhoo rigged on Number 12 (200-lb. test) single strand wire.
We were pulling them on 80-pound test
monofilament outfits and .035 (80-pound
test) Monel wire line outfits.

Upon closer inspection of our skirted
ballyhoo baits, however, that's where the
"basics" ended; each bait featured a long
shank lead hook positioned back by the
anal vent, and a slightly smaller, shorter
shank, free-swinging hook with its point

riding upward. The latter is the "stinger"
hook, and it rode alongside the bait's tail. I
affectionately dubbed this set-up the "Cayman Crusher", after it "cleaned house"
during our shoot. It is a standard among
serious wahoo anglers in the Caymans,
as well as with accomplished tournament
competitors the likes of Chris Briggs and
Charles Ebanks.

There are a few components
which enable the Cayman Crusher to
wreak havoc on fish. To begin with, the
positioning of the lead hook so far aft
tends to foil short-striking fish. And if
for some reason the lead hook doesn't
"stick", that stinger hook will! In several instances, both hooks were deeply
imbedded into the jaws of wahoo; an
"insurance" of sorts against fish shaking
them free. Additionally, when trolled,
the free-swinging stinger hook "flutters"
alongside the ballyhoo's tail; this emits
a "vibration" fish key in on, and creates
the illusion of the bait's tail "beating/
kicking" frantically as it tries to escape
predation. Then, of course, there's the

Few wahoo can escape the "hold" put on them by the Cayman Crusher!

CARE FOR THOSE BAITS PROPERLY

When rigging numerous baits for a few days of offshore trolling, I keep them organized on aluminum baits trays made by Engel-USA, and stored in my Engel cooler. These powder-coated aluminum bait trays run two- to three-inches deep, and stack on top of each other. The aluminum keeps the baits cold and dry, as melted ice seeps through the drains in the trays.

Even with bait trays sitting on top of a layer of ice, it's still necessary to care for those baits. Here's how I do it:

Step 1 - Layer the bottom of a cooler with a few bags of ice (exact number of bags will reflect the size of cooler, but you want the ice to fill at least 1/4 of the cooler).

Step 2 - Liberally sprinkle kosher salt onto the ice, which brings the temperature of the melting ice and subsequent brine to near freezing.

Step 3 - Layer several baits on the tray – backs down and bellies up. Then, add a sprinkling of kosher salt and baking soda (which preserves the color and freshness of the baits), followed by a light sprinkling of ice.

Step 4 – Repeat the steps outlined above until you've stacked the amount of bait trays you anticipate using.

TIPS:

a.) Make sure the baits always have some ice on top of them, to keep them moist and from spoiling.

b.) On the way offshore, place the "starting line up" of baits in a bucket of sea water, so they'll be thoroughly thawed and limber, and ready to catch fish.

streamlined and brilliance appearance of the Ilander skirt, which adds "flash" and realism, in addition to preventing the ballyhoo from washing out at brisk trolling speeds.

Here's how Eric Rivers rigs the Cayman Crusher:

Step one: He'll attach the lead hook, either a 10/0 or 11/0 (based on bait size), to the leader with numerous haywire twists. The exact number of "twists" is determined by laying the hook alongside the ballyhoo, and lining up its point with the bait's anal cavity. He'll want as many "twists" as it takes to go from the eye of the hook to the bait's lower jaw. When the Haywire twists are completed, he'll lock them in place with a barrel wrap, break off the wire "tag", and secure a strand of soft rigging wire to the leader. He'll then form a small loop in the leader's opposite end, for the trolling outfit's snap swivel.

Step two: After creating the main leader, he'll fabricate the stinger rig. The exact length of this attachment is determined by laying the bend of the stinger hook alongside and even with the bait's tail, and determining the amount of cable needed to span from the eye of the stinger hook, to the eye of the lead hook. He'll then make sure the hook point rides upright, in contrast to the point of the lead hook, which rides point down. Next, the stinger hook is crimped to 480-lb test cable (using 1/16 sleeves). Then, the cable is crimped to the eye of the lead hook, off to the side of the main leader and opposite of where the lead hook's "eye" compresses into its shank; securing the stinger cable on this side greatly lessens the risk of it forcing open the lead hook's eye, when battling a fish.

Step three: With the complete rig intact,

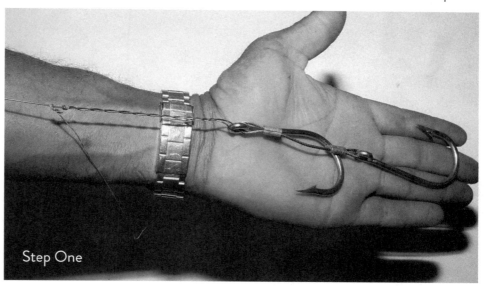

Step One

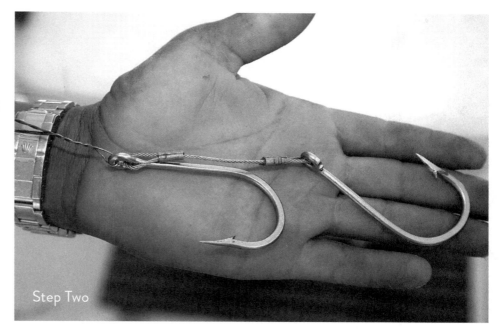

Step Two

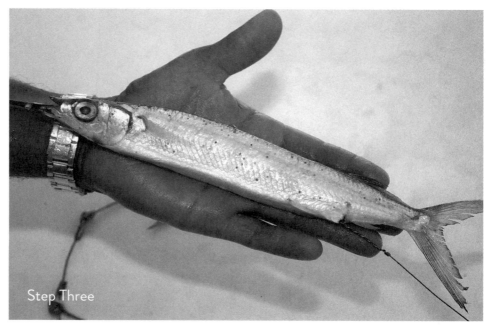

Step Three

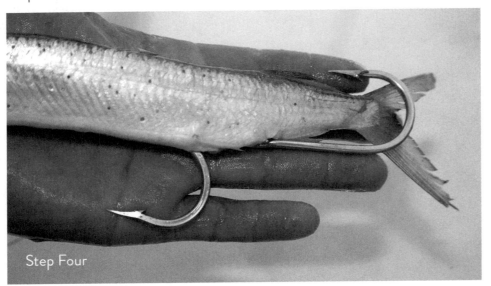

Step Four

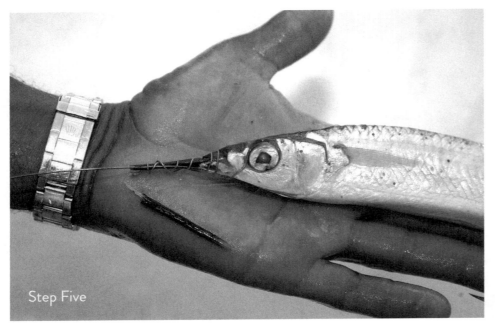

Step Five

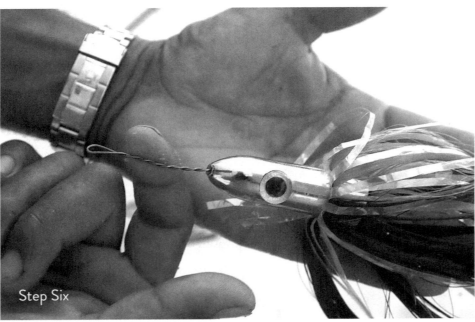

Step Six

minus the skirt, Eric then inserts the top of the leader into the ballyhoo's anal vent, "snakes" it up through the body cavity and out the center of the throat latch.

Step four: He'll pull the leader through the bait, until the eye and shank of the lead hook are snugged up inside the anal cavity, and the "stinger" hook is dangling outside the bait.

Step five: He'll secure the bait to the leader by initially running the soft wire through the bait's eyes, followed by a series of tight wraps going forward - around both jaws and leader.

Step six: To complete the rig, he slides an Ilander lure onto the leader, and over the baits snout. However, it's necessary to first drill a larger opening on the Ilander skirt, so that the leader loop can pass through. Nearly all his Ilander skirts have been drilled out for this purpose.

Eric says the ability to quickly change skirt colors is important to him and a lot of wahoo anglers; they can do so in a matter of seconds with this rig. And seeing these rigs in action and the wahoo we caught on them, I've got to tip my white visor to the Cayman Crusher! ✻

The author with a wahoo that fell victim to the Cayman Crusher!

When running offshore, the author keeps a watchful eye on his radar for birds. His radar frequently leads him to the birds, which, in turn, uncover the fish.

Chapter 22
Using Electronics to Catch More Fish!
Make your electronics lead you to fish!

Serious salt water anglers are always seeking an edge when it comes to catching fish, and modern marine electronics have certainly made it easier for us to at least find them.

There are countless features offered by modern radars, fish finders, GPS and electronic chart systems. So much so, that I'm astounded over how much navigation and fish-finding technology can be incorporated into today's small- and mid-size boats; reaching far away destinations has never been so precise or safe, and it's certainly not as easy for game fish to sneak under the radar – no pun intended.

Despite the full capabilities of my electronics package on my Mako 284 center console, I rely immensely on five basic features when I head to sea. I've learned to really fine-tune and read these features, to where I can consistently locate fish, and even save fuel in the process. Listed below are the five items I can't fish without, along with a look at how I dial them in to find action aboard my MARC VI:

Radar
Radar is first and foremost a major safety addition, and I've relied on mine

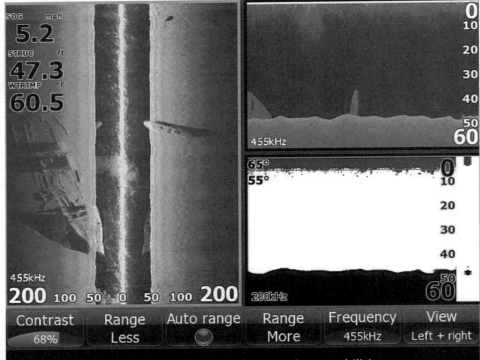

StructureScan by Lowrance lends side-scanning capabilities to a vessel, as well as Down Scan. In this image, the wreck and related bottom structure is to the left of the vessel (left screen), whereas the wreck is evident on the Down Scan reading (upper right), and on the fish finder reading (lower right). Note the sharpness and video-like view of these objects in StructureScan.

There's no substitute for a quality fish finder, particularly when bottom fishing. Pictured here is a fat blackfish, which was caught by precisely anchoring the boat over a prime piece of structure.

numerous times to safely navigate around and through bad thunderstorms, and when running at night.

However, even on those bluebird days, if I'm offshore trolling, my radar is on and helping me look for birds. Once a luxury on big sportfishing boats, powerful radars and fairly large open array antennas are now common on small- and mid-size boats. I've a 4kW unit with a four-foot open array antenna (7-degree horizontal beam width & 25-degree vertical beam width); it's important to remember that open array antennas, compared to closed dome systems, are more conducive to "bird watching".

I'll select a range of six miles, and nearly max out the gain. Any bird activity appears as small and light reddish "blotches" or marks on the screen. When there are just one or two birds, the capture on the radar is so small, an inexperienced eye might overlook it. However, major gatherings of birds appear as larger, darker markings, which, obviously, are more easily distinguished. The trick is to monitor that "blotch" or mark and wait for the antennae to sweep around a couple times; if that blotch or mark still appears on the screen, head to it – those are the birds!

Plotters

I love it when South Florida dolphin anglers tell me how they trolled south nearly all day, covered a ton of ground, and didn't do well. Off South Florida, for instance, many anglers troll in a southerly fashion, to keep the northbound Gulf Stream from sweeping them far north of their home inlet, and making for a long run home. However, if a boat trolls around five- or six-knots directly or nearly directly into the Gulf Stream, which flows between four and seven knots on average, they're not covering a lot of ground, like they may suspect, just water! This is somewhat similar with the Loop Current in the Gulf and the mid-Atlantic and Northeast eddies.

When I'm trolling, I'll activate my chart plotter and its trail feature; this shows the boat's precise position on that chart and the ground I'm covering. Therefore, I know my exact whereabouts when working along contour lines, major structures, humps, depressions, ledges, etc. In addition, when a significant water surface temperature break is noted, or we get a strike or catch a quality fish, I'll mark that spot and spend time working the immediate vicinity.

As for covering both ground and water in a strong current, such as the Gulf Stream, I often troll a broad zig-zag, shallow-to-deep pattern, rather than directly into the current, or with it.

Also, when bottom fishing, we can quickly determine if there's a current by zooming in on the plotter and watching the boat's movement. If there's no current, it saves us the effort of anchoring and valuable fishing time.

Structure Scan

My Lowrance HDS units feature the company's StructureScan option. This is basically side-imaging sonar, where I can program the distances I wish to scan off both the port and starboard side of my vessel, or just any one side. In addition, there's also Down Scan, which, similar to the fish finder, shoots downward. But the big difference here is that it yields highly-detailed images of the ocean floor along with any bait and game fish.

StructureScan gives me a picture-quality view through the waters surrounding the boat, and also beneath it. Ledges, drop-offs, rock piles, structure, bait, game fish, suspended debris,

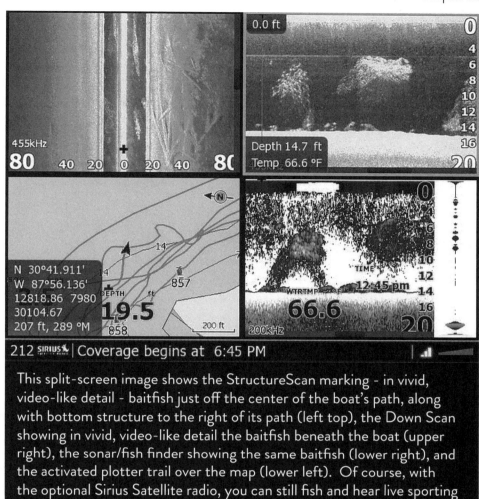

This split-screen image shows the StructureScan marking - in vivid, video-like detail - baitfish just off the center of the boat's path, along with bottom structure to the right of its path (left top), the Down Scan showing in vivid, video-like detail the baitfish beneath the boat (upper right), the sonar/fish finder showing the same baitfish (lower right), and the activated plotter trail over the map (lower left). Of course, with the optional Sirius Satellite radio, you can still fish and hear live sporting events, or your favorite tunes!

By using a quality fish finder, especially with StructureScan, you'll easily uncover the whereabouts of fish, such as these schooling yellowtail snapper.

Radar is a must-have item, if you're serious at catching offshore fish, like this yellowfin tuna. Radar also leads inshore and near shore anglers to the birds, which uncover game fish like striped bass, bluefish, mackerel, etc.

etc. appear as if I had a video camera down there. What's more, I can even identify certain species of fish.

I use it when bottom fishing, to locate wrecks, structure and even fish-whereabouts. In one instance, I was anchored on a favorite yellowtail spot off Bimini, and had Cero mackerel, Horse-eye jacks, amberjack, barracuda and sharks stacked up in the chum slick behind my boat – but no yellowtails. After two hours of catching a lot of fish, I thought it was odd we didn't see any yellowtail.

I turned on my StructureScan, and set the side views out to 40 feet; I noticed a large school of yellowtail 35 feet off the port side of the boat, just about in-line with my console. They were schooling up there, to avoid being eaten by the jacks, 'cudas and sharks behind the boat. I pitched a bait to the school, and began catching yellowtail. If it wasn't for StructureScan revealing those fish, we would have missed out on them.

It's also great for drifting or trolling the reefs, as we can uncover new spots, see where the bait and fish are schooling, and even watch any bottom baits or jigs we're dropping. And should we see a spot we'd like to save, the TrackBack feature enables me to scroll back the sonar and chart plotter "history" to set waypoints and share

them across the network. The StructureScan transducer is separate to the one for the sonar, and there's also the option of a transom mount or thru-hull transducer.

Zoom Feature

When bottom fishing in particular, I'll split the screen on my fishfinder: one side shows the full depth range, the other just the last 20 feet of the water column.

This "Zoom" feature expands the view of the bottom, providing a clear, concise image of the structure, as well as any bait or game fish concentrations. If the bottom appears void of life, despite how good the structure might appear, I'll move either deeper or shallower along that zone, or to another reef. Over wrecks, we'll have a sharp view of the structure as well as the sections holding bait and game fish.

The full view side of the screen will uncover any bait or pelagics in the mid to upper water column, equally important when trolling or drifting along the reefs and over deep, offshore structure. Furthermore, we can detect the thermocline, an important consideration when drifting baits for swordfish, sharks and even tuna.

Electronic Charts

Offshore anglers are a structure-ori-

ented bunch; we're always searching for "suspended" structure - which includes weedlines, floating debris, rips, significant water surface temperature breaks, etc., and prominent bottom structure – such as deep depth contours, dramatic drop offs, sea mounts, wrecks, etc.

While "suspended" structure requires our eyes to locate, there are premium versions of electronic charts which explicitly show in great detail the bottom make up of a specific area, or region. This includes highly detailed contour lines as well as major structure and even some wrecks.

These charts take the guess work out of locating potentially productive zones to fish, and are extremely helpful when visiting destinations where you don't have a lot of "local" knowledge.

If I'm heading out to troll offshore, for example, I'll study the chart for where specific deep fathom curves run closest together. I'll then place the cursor on that spot, cruise to the area and begin trolling. These "tight" contour lines reveal a quickly descending bottom, opposed to a gradual bottom decline (typical of contour lines that lay farther apart from each other). Should a strong current wash over these zones, upwellings and concentrations of bait could exist – and yield good fishing.

What's more, any new finds we locate can be added to our chart. Over time, we've acquired a "circuit" of structures that we can systematically target based on tides, current, etc. And when we're at these spots, our plotter's trail feature is activated.

If you study that fish finder and StructureScan, keep track of your boat's position over quality bottom charts, and watch the radar for birds, you'll find that locating fish doesn't get any easier! ✳

The author's new MARC VI - a tricked-out, newly redesigned Mako 284 - on the troll off the Bahamas.

Tricking Out a Center Console

Center console fishing boats are the backbone of the recreational saltwater fishing market, ranging from a simple 17-footer used for trout, redfish, striped bass and bluefish, on up to a tricked out 33-footer rigged for serious offshore fishing. There's no denying their effectiveness, and one can only imagine how many impressive fish these boats have produced since they first came on the market.

My new MARC VI is a 2011, newly-reengineered, Mako 284 center console, which showcases just how dialed

in for fishing these boats can be. The 284, incidentally, is the flagship of the company's fleet and one of the best-selling models ever for Mako. The 284 is actually 28-feet, 4-inches in length. The hull sports a 21-degree dead rise - which provides a soft and quick ride through agitated seas, whereas its spacious 9-foot, 10-inch beam provides remarkable stability while trolling, at drift or on anchor. The reengineered hull features a one-piece integrated stringer grid with molded gelcoat finish. There is no wood, and the hull

comes in around 800-pounds lighter than its predecessor.

The 284 features a new wide and cushioned leaning post complete with lockable storage and backrest with rod racks. The bait prep station sports a 50-gallon redesigned live well, fed by a 1,650 GPH pump. The back up - or secondary pump is a 1,100 GPH unit. To prevent overflowing from the influx of additional water, a second, larger-diameter drain was added to the well. The drains are sufficient enough to keep up with the influx of fresh seawa-

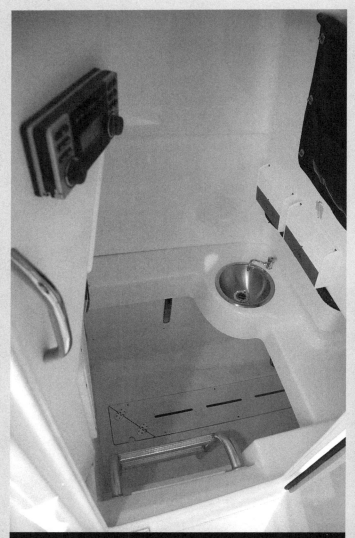

Internal console space is abundant on the 2011 MARC VI. Porta-Potty was removed by Poveromo to provide even more storage space. Note the fixed ladder leading into the console.

The bait prep station sports a 50-gallon redesigned live well, fed by a 1,650 GPH pump. The back up - or secondary pump is a 1,100 GPH unit.

The MARC VI is equipped with Lee 16-foot Sidewinder outriggers and a Lee Center rigger.

Each Lee outrigger pole is rigged with two independent and adjustable cords, allowing two baits to be deployed per pole.

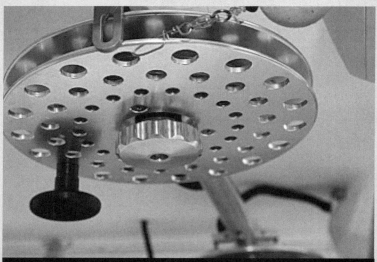

A pair of Elec-Tra-Mate TR 300 Teezer Reels enable the new MARC VI to deploy a range of surface teasers. Each reel has a "clicker" that can be activated, for audible warnings of any line slippage.

ter. And to keep the live well operating overnight at a marina without taxing the batteries, there's a 110 Volt battery charger mounted inside the console. Other notable leaning post items include a removable cutting board, tackle storage, and sink with on-demand freshwater.

The all-new center console sports digital gauges, an oversized electronics mounting surface, recessed and covered electrical switches, grab rail and forward-console seat with insulated and self-draining cooler. I removed the stock glass windshield and instead had Action Canvas install a full Strata-Glass weather enclosure. Inside, there's a fully-lined head enclosure.

In deck are two insulated, 390-quart fish boxes with dedicated diaphragm drainage, The bilge is extremely easy to access, and here you'll find a redundant bilge pump system with dual 2,000 GPH pumps. In-deck water channels and large cockpit drains keep the deck dry, no mater how wet the weather or high the seas.

Looking to go a bit beyond the standard Mako layout and options, I modified my boat more toward my style of fishing. It should be noted that a lot of these modifications are not factory options, and credit must go to John Bower and his team at Mako for incorporating these modifications into the boat.

TROLLING

I ordered Mako's custom deluxe hard-top (versus the standard fabric top), and had it outfitted with Lee Side-winder outriggers, and a Lee center rigger. The 16-foot, Lee Sidewinder Extra Strong poles are deployed and retrieved by turning their handles, which are located beneath the top; the poles swing out and lock in at an 80-degree trolling position. The attitude of the

poles can also be raised or lowered (0, 30 or 60 degrees) by simply pushing down on their collars, at their bases. These features enable quick deployment and retrieval of the outriggers, and to even raise them or lay them flat and parallel with the top for clearing low bridges and when trailering. The 16-foot Lee center rigger is fixed in its position; I remove that pole for trailering. Each of the three Lee poles are rigged with two independent cords and release clips. In all, I can troll six baits from the poles on my T-top.

Six, 30-degree angle, Lee Rod Holders were mounted in the cockpit gunwales. Of the three units per side, the ones farthest aft (aimed directly seaward) are Lee Flush Mounted Rod Holders. The ones right behind them are Lee Swivel Rod Holders, and the ones right behind those (angled outward 10-degrees) are Lee Flush Mounted Rod Holders. Add in the four rod holders behind the console seat and the MARC VI can easily troll up to ten rods. The reason for the Swivel Rod Holders, incidentally, is for heavy duty fishing with bent butt rods - such as wire line trolling for grouper and wahoo, and daytime swordfishing.

Since we do a lot of run-and-gun fishing for dolphin, and for when a school of dolphin is encountered, our light tackle outfits must be readily accessible. Most of this tackle rides in the five aft T-top rod holders. Two additional T-top rod holders were added to the forward T-top (one on each side), so that an angler up front won't have to scramble back behind the console to grab a rod. A total of seven rods can be racked along the T-top, all rigged to cover a variety of fishing opportunities.

To compliment the outriggers and my trolling, I installed a pair of Elec-Tra-Mate TR 310 Teezer Reels. These reels are machined from solid

6061 T-6 aircraft marine aluminum and are affixed to the underside of my T-top, with the line from the port-side reel running up through the far eye on the port outrigger, and the line from the starboard reel running up through the far eye on my starboard outrigger. Each Teezer reel holds 300 feet of 300-pound test monofilament. What's more, each reel has a "clicker" that can be activated, which alerts the crew when a teaser is slipping back, or a fish has struck one. From the dual Teezer reels, I usually position a large, 18 – 21-inch long, hookless marlin teaser between 10- and 20-feet behind the boat On the opposite side, and roughly the same distance back, I run a Williamson squid spreader bar (I occasionally change out these teasers with Williamson mullet daisy chains, particularly when dolphin trolling). From there, I position my close baits within five feet or so of the teasers, and stagger the remaining baits back from there. To enhance my teaser set-up, I also pull two 6-arm 104-fish StripTeaser Dredges, one from each transom corner. The dredges ride roughly 15 feet and 4 to 6 feet beneath the surface.

LIVE BAITING

Since we also do a lot of live-baiting for sails and kings, we had eight additional Lee Flush Mounted Rod Holders positioned in the mid-ship and forward gunwales (four per side). These holders are aimed directly seaward, since we primarily drift. In addition, these 15-degree angle holders keep their rods nearly vertical and off the bow rail. When we slow troll live baits, we'll use the cockpit rod holders. Between the cockpit-based rod holders, and those in the mid-ship and bow, the MARC VI has 14 gunwale-based rod holders.

Kite fishing is a specialty of ours,

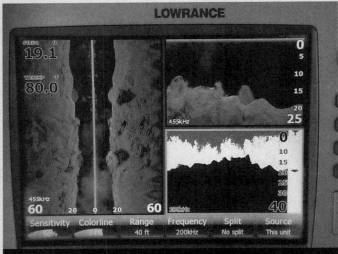

The MARC VI features Structure Scan by Lowrance, which provides side imaging as well as down scan. Here, the MARC VI uncovers a wreck off the Abacos, during a recent trip.

Between the four holders in the new leaning post and tackle prep module and the seven holders on the T-Top, the MARC VI can keep 11 rods within quick reach.

The new MARC VI features a state-of-the-art JL Audio system, with precision-arranged speakers and subwoofers.

A pair of Lowrance VHF radios rest in the overhead E-box. Each VHF is rigged to its own antenna.

A pair of JL Audio M-Series amplifiers are housed within the console of the MARC VI.

A very impressive and highly functional Lowrance electronics package is flush-mounted within the big Mako console. This includes fish finders, mapping systems, GPS, StructureScan, Sirius satellite weather and even a SIMRAD autopilot.

and we often deploy a kite from both the cockpit and bow. To power the electric kite reel in the cockpit, a power outlet is recessed under the aft starboard gunwale. The outlet for the bow-based kite reel is mounted within the anchor locker and to the underside of the bow platform. To use this outlet without having to remove the anchor locker cover, a "channel" was carved into the upper port side of the hatch cover. The diameter of this "channel" is also large enough for anchor line to pass.

BOTTOM FISHING

As mentioned earlier, the Lee Swivel Rod Holders accommodate our wire line outfits for grouper trolling and day swordfishing, whereas the rod holders spread about the gunwales take care of any additional rods we set into action. When it's time to hunker up against the gunwales and lean into a big fish, the full 360-degree coaming bolster - a Mako standard on the 284, is easy on the thighs.

An anchor retrieval ball, two 300-foot sections of 3/4-inch rode, 18-feet of chain and an anchor are housed within the forward anchor locker, along with dock lines. Beneath the center deck hatch are the spare anchor and retrieval ball and docking fenders.

THE ELECTRONICS PACKAGE

The MARC VI has a very impressive and highly functional Lowrance package. Two Lowrance HDS-10 (High Definition System) units and one Lowrance HDS-8 unit are flush-mounted in the big Mako console. Each HDS-10 unit is a high definition, color fish finder/GPS Chart Plotter and radar. Although each function above can be independently displayed on the 10.4-inch screen - or in split screen mode, I prefer keeping the fish finder fully dis-

played on one unit and the mapping system or radar up on the other unit.

The Lowrance HDS-8 is a totally independent unit, complete with a dual frequency Skimmer transom-mount transducer. This unit pretty much serves as a back up system, although it will show everything the HDS-10 units will, including radar.

To get clear and concise bottom readings to 3,000 feet from the HDS-10 units, we opted for a special-order, AIRMAR bronze, through hull, 1,000 kilowatts rms, 50/200 kHz transducer (model B260), and flush-mounted it into the hull.

In addition, the units have Lowrance's new Structure Scan option. This enables me to not only read the bottom straight beneath my boat (down scan), but also off to the sides of my vessel at programmable distances. This side-imaging has proven extremely helpful in finding bait and game fish, wrecks, and unique structure within inlets and channels and along bridges. Structure Scan gives a video-like image that is clear and quite remarkable. Also an option, I selected the new thru-hull Structure Scan transducer, over the transom mount 'ducer.

This should read: As mentioned, the HDS-10 units have 4kw radar capabilities, and I've paired mine with the LRA 5000 – a 4-foot, open array antennae. The power of the radar in conjunction with the open array antennae has proven helpful in picking up bird activity and, of course, navigating through thunderstorms and heavy rains.

All three Lowrance units display SIRIUS Satellite Weather, a huge advantage for keeping safe on the water. And on the topic of safety, two Lowrance VHF radios are flush-mounted inside the electronics box,

each rigged to its own 8-foot Shake-speare antennae.

ROCK AND ROLL TIME

The MARC VI has an incredible stereo system designed exclusively for it by JL Audio. The head unit is a Clarion MW1 stereo complete with Sirius satellite radio. From there, it's all JL Audio.

SPEAKERS

There are three pairs (six speakers) of JL Audio model MX770-CG-WH full range speakers. These speakers are designed and engineered for heavy duty marine use and greatly exceed industry standards for salt-fog and UV exposure. Needless to say, corrosion and UV-resistant materials are prominent throughout. Acoustics-wise, the speakers are engineered to deliver a powerful, clean sound in open-air boat environments (i.e. center consoles). They feature 0.75-inch silk dome tweeters for sparkling high frequency detail, whereas a long excursion, high-efficiency woofer design delivers impressive bass energy and clean mid-range. They're designed to benefit from operation with quality amplifiers up to 125W per channel.

SUBWOOFERS

The MARC VI has two JL Audio model MX10IB3-4-CG-WH subwoofers. These subwoofer drivers are engineered to withstand the rigors of marine use and deliver the kind of bass that has made JL Audio famous in the automotive sound arena. This bass will not only impress you with its sheer level, but also its smoothness, balance and precision. Equally impressive, especially for center console owners, is that the MX10IB3-4-CG-WH is optimized for infinite-baffle operation so that it can be installed in a variety of locations, without the need for a dedicated enclosure.

There are two insulated, 390-quart fish boxes with dedicated diaphragm drainage in the new Mako 284. In one box, Poveromo keeps his cleaning brushes and gaffs.

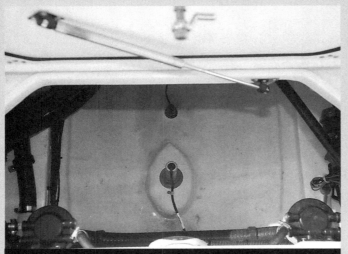

The new Mako 284 sports easy access to the bilge and vital components.

An all new center console on the Mako 284 offers plenty of space for electronics, as well as recessed and covered electrical switches. The MARC VI also sports a custom SeaDek helm pad.

Twin Mercury Verado 300hp outboards power the MARC VI. The new, supercharged, Verados are 20% more fuel efficient than its predecessors. A pair of 21-pitch Mercury Vengeance props help deliver a top-speed of 57-miles per hour at 6,200 rpms.

In deck are two insulated, 390-quart fish boxes with dedicated diaphragm drainage, one of which is pictured here and caring for the day's catch aboard the MARC VI.

AMPLIFIERS

One M600/6 - a 600 watt, 6-channel full range amplifier which drives all six of the MX770-CCX-CG-WH speakers, and one M600/1 - a 600 watt mono-block subwoofer amplifier, round out the system. The JL Audio M-Series amplifiers are amazingly small in size and the perfect solution for space-conscious installations. Furthermore, JL Audio's exclusive NexD switching technology achieves total amplifier efficiencies exceeding 80%; this means far less heat and strain on your vessel's electrical system, compared to a large, conventional amplifier. This efficiency advantage, combined with state-of-the-art microelectronic components, allows JL Audio to use very compact unitary cast alloy heat sinks. As with their more expensive MHD siblings, the M-Series also deploy the company's Advanced Thermal Rollback System, to completely eliminate annoying thermal shut-down events.

Behind every M-Series amplifier's removable control cover, you will find studio-grade signal processing with fully variable crossover filters. Also included are noise-killing, differential inputs with remote level control capabilities via the HD-RLC remote level control (optional).

The volume, crispness and clarity of this system is concert-like, particularly when "cranked up"! There is no distortion, just sharp and clear audio that will rival the best home-based sound systems. JL Audio wanted the new MARC VI to "make a statement" with its sound system, and it does exactly that. It has to be heard to really be appreciated!

To insure there's enough power for all these electronics, the MARC VI has four batteries. One is mounted underneath the seating module, whereas the remaining three are flush-mounted inside the inner console's fire wall. Inside the console, you'll find battery switches and circuit breaker panels. There's six feet of head room here and a lockable door - ideal for securing your rods overnight at a marina or in a hotel parking lot. An ACR GlobalFix 406 EPIRB with Integral GPS is also located here, within easy reach, as are two fire extinguishers. A dual-color LED light (white or blue) illuminates the console at night.

LIT UP AND READY TO RUN

A pair of halogen lights integrated into the aft T-top brighten up the entire cockpit, while a single halogen light on the forward T-top takes care of the bow area. In lieu of a fluorescent T-top light, the MARC VI has five LED courtesy lights recessed into the bottom of the electronics box; two lights are white and three are blue - with independent switches. The boat also has blue LED lighting at the base of the console and underneath the gunwales.

For night-fishing, the MARC VI was outfitted with four Shadow Caster Marine LED lights, in "Bimini Blue". Model SCM-10v-BB20 provides over 2000 lumens/42 Watts of high intensity lighting with a lamp life expectancy of 40,000 hours. The lights rely on an internal digital switching power supply, and operate at 94% efficiency while drawing a mere 3.5 amps at 12 volts. The compact and sleek lights are framed in chrome and lend a sharp look to the boat, especially when it's on the trailer.

ALL THE POWER AND THEN SOME

My new MARC VI is powered by a pair of Mercury Verado, 300-horsepower outboards. The new generation Verados are extremely powerful, quiet, and 20% more fuel efficient than their predecessors. What's more, the new Verados can now run on regular gasoline to make their maximum horsepower, versus hi-test in the past. The MARC VI's power is harnessed by a pair of 21-pitch Mercury Vengeance props, which deliver a top-speed of 57-miles per hour at 6,200 rpms. The hole shot performance is breathtaking, whereas the outboards "sweet" and most fuel efficient cruise rpm – as verified on the Mercury SmartCraft fuel management system - is 3,800 rpms. Mercury's Digital Throttle & Shift system provides precise acceleration and ease of operation, whereas the power steering system makes handling the boat an enjoyable experience.

GETTING HER TO THE DANCE

To haul the MARC VI to and from the local ramp, as well as to various coastal cities along the U.S. when shooting for our VERSUS television show, we rely on a custom-built trailer from the FLOAT-ON Corporation in Vero Beach, Florida. The aluminum, I-Beam, immersible, dual-axle trailer is rated for 12,700-pounds and features a hot-dipped, galvanized torsion axle suspension (a FLOAT-ON exclusive for over 30 years). It is equipped with 16-inch radial tires, hydraulic surge disc brakes with booted bronze pistons and stainless steel rotors (for increased braking performance and longer life), PVC-covered heavy-aluminum guide rails for centering the boat on the trailer, LED lights, and reflective decals for higher visibility and safer travelling in low light conditions, or at night. FLOAT-ON is an industry leader in the boat trailer business, and the only trailer worthy of carrying the MARC VI.

From T-top to trailer, this is the sweetest and most functional MARC VI to date! I love it - and game fish should fear it! ❋

FEATURING

GORE GORE® Performance Fiber

ALWAYS
USE THE BEST
LINE™

New X-Rap® Magnum® 05

Seafood's seafood.

Dist NM
5.65

hrs
11:16

30   60

Speed kn
0.3

HDG °M
032

CONFIDENCE TO GO
WHERE THE BILLFISH ARE BITING

INTRODUCING THE NEW NSS EVO2

This is the system you've been waiting for. It combines the ease of a tablet-style, multi-touch screen with the precision control of a push-to-select, rotary knob for rolling seas. We call it Touch Sensible — you'll call it amazing.

Add in our Simrad exclusive, dedicated, power-cruising screens, the widest available fish-finding technologies on the market, industry-leading integration capabilities and stylish, low-profile, flush-mount design and you can see why this is the most enticing cruising and fishing system on the market.

So whatever your destination, you can be confident the Simrad NSS evo2 can get you there like no one else. **For more information go to simrad-yachting.com/sws.**

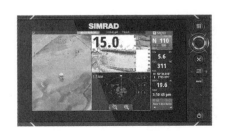

Go With Confidence

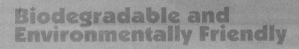

COME FISH BIMINI!

BIMINI SANDS RESORT & MARINA

Luxury resort and deepwater marina located directly on the beach overlooking the famous Bimini color change. Choose your passion - fishing, diving or just getting away from it all. Bimini Sands also offers guided eco-tours including kayaking, snorkeling, shark dives and much more. See you at the Sands!

Nightlife

Oceanfront

Dining

Luxury

For reservations please call 1.242.347.3500 or visit us online at www.biminisands.com

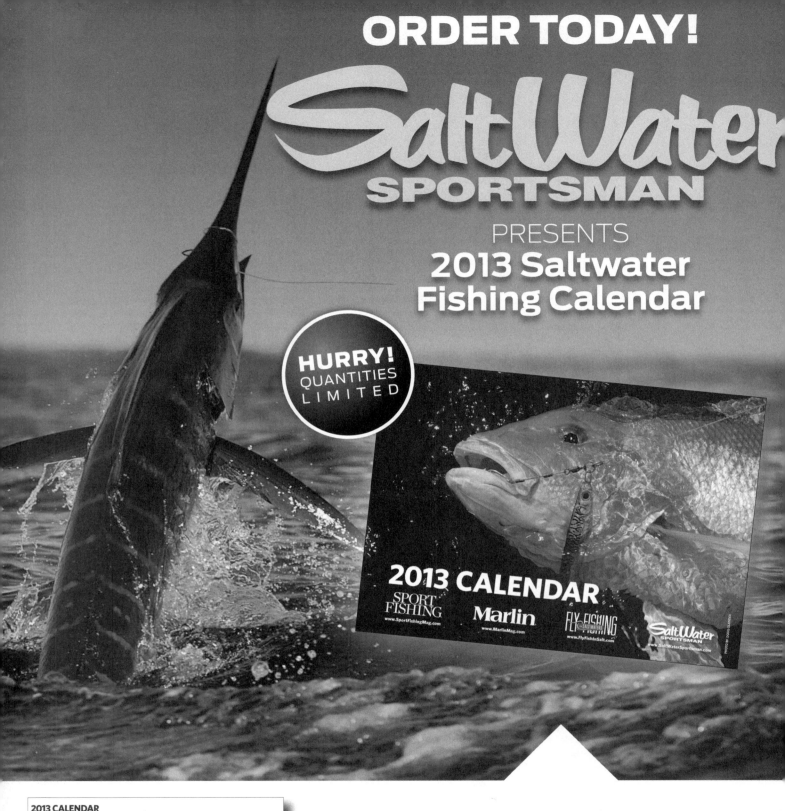

CATCH MORE FISH

WITH ROFFS™ OCEANOGRAPHIC FISHING ANALYSES

2013 HIGHLIGHTS:
474 TOURNAMENT WINNERS

STATE RECORDS:
ALABAMA BLUE MARLIN
NEW YORK WAHOO

TOURNAMENT WINNERS
SOUTH CAROLINA GOVERNOR'S CUP
NORTH CAROLINA GOVERNOR'S CUP
SOUTHERN KINGFISH DIVISON V
OCEAN CITY WHITE MARLIN OPEN
MID-ATLANTIC $500,000
TRI-STATE CANYON SHOOTOUT
OAK BLUFFS SHARK
QUEST FOR THE CREST
TEXAS INTERNATIONAL FISH TOURN.
NORTHEAST FLORIDA WAHOO

**PINPOINTS HOT SPOTS
TELLS HOW MANY DAYS
THE OCEAN CONDITIONS
HAVE BEEN FAVORABLE**

CATCH REPORTS

**FREE UPDATES
WHILE FISHING**

**CURRENT EDGES
SHOWS WATER COLOR
WATER TEMPERATURE
BOTTOM TOPOGRAPHY
NAVIGATIONAL COORDINATES**

**COMPREHENSIVE ANALYSIS:
MAP AND TEXT DESCRIPTION**

**WHY GUESS WITH INTERNET
IMAGES OR OTHER IMITATIONS**

**EVERY FISHING TRIP IS IMPORTANT - WWW.ROFFS.COM
TOLL FREE 800 677-7633 & 321 723-5759**

ROFFER'S OCEAN FISHING FORECASTING SERVICE, INC.

TOLL FREE 800 677-7633 // 321 723-5759 // WWW.ROFFS.COM

SALT WATER SPORTSMAN SEMINAR SERIES

PRESENT THIS GIFT CERTIFICATE FOR ONE FREE
ROFFS™ FISHING OCEANOGRAPHIC ANALYSIS FOR OFFSHORE FISHING

THIS ENTITLES YOU TO ONE PERSONALIZED FISHING FORECASTING ANALYSIS WHICH WILL IDENTIFY THE OFFSHORE AREAS WHERE BILLFISH, TUNA, SHARKS, MAHI, KINGFISH, AND OTHER FISH ARE LIKELY TO BE CONCENTRATED. GOOD FOR ANY ROFFS™ FORECAST AREA AND SENT VIA TELPHONE FACSIMILE OR COLOR EMAIL. THIS INCLUDES A FULL PAGE OCEAN FRONTAL ANALYSIS CHART AND A WRITTEN DISCUSSION OF THE CURRENT AND FORECAST FISHING CONDITIONS.

MUST BE USED BETWEEN 01 MARCH AND DATES BELOW PER AREA

THIS CERTIFICATE MUST BE SUBMITTED (FAX, EMAIL, MAIL) PRIOR TO USE
MUST CALL AT LEAST 24 HOURS IN ADVANCE TO ORDER

1. **New Bern, NC: Use by July 05, 2014**
2. **Uncasville, CT: Use by July 15, 2014**
3. **Long Branch, NJ: Use by July 15, 2014**
4. **Annapolis, MD: Use by July 15, 2014**

5. **Tavernier, FL: Use by May 31, 2014**
6. **Pasadena, TX: Use By July 15, 2014**
7. **Columbia, SC: Use By July 05, 2014**
8. **Ponte Vedra, FL: Use by July 05, 2014**

AUTHORIZED BY

Mitchell a Roffer

MITCHELL A. ROFFER, PH.D.
PRESIDENT

AUTHORIZATION NUMBER

13347MaR@60West

Your Name   Boat Name   Telephone Number

NEW Raku Jig

Easy Does It.

**Translated, Raku means "easy" and this lure earns the name.
Cast and swim. Drop and jig. Deadstick in moving current.
Raku's articulated body and dual action proves irresistible.**

for the Pelagic Playground™

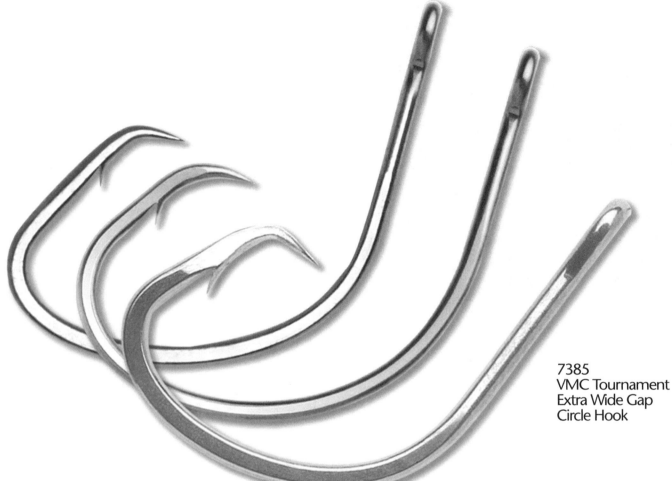

7385
VMC Tournament
Extra Wide Gap
Circle Hook

GEORG
POVEROM

I USE VMC
CIRCLE HOOKS

NEVER SET THE HOOK. With Circle Hooks the "Hook Set" is accomplished through pressure, not strike force. As the hook rotates in the fish's mouth, the line comes tight as the hook penetrates resulting in an increased survival rate among our challenged fish population.

Your Expert In Hooks

www.vmchooks.com

(855) 822-5539

· **Perfect for T-Tops, platforms, railings, seats and more...**
· **Secure easy storage.**
· **Marine Grade / UV Bonded.**
· **"V" series hook and loop mounted bags are perfect for keeping hatches organized.**

"TackleWebs are suspending tackle storage systems that are ideal for keeping terminal gear and other items organized and accessible within seconds. I use them on my MARC VI."
George Poveromo – Renowned saltwater angler, writer and television host.

TACKLE WEBS™

SUSPENDING STORAGE SYSTEM

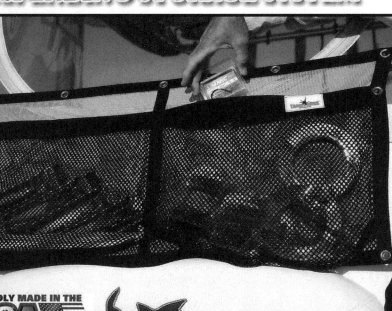

PROUDLY MADE IN THE USA

www.TACKLEWEBS.com

FIND. NAVIGATE.
DOMINATE.

Find more hot spots.

- Built-in StructureScan® HD for photo-like sidescan and DownScan Imaging™ views
- Broadband Sounder® for unmatched detail
- DownScan Overlay™, delivering greater fish and structure validation
- TrackBack™, now with a preview pane, for quicker access to sonar history

Navigate with enhanced mapping tools.

- Build custom maps with Insight Genesis™
- Experience built-in 3D Insight™ mapping
- View Navionics® and Insight™ charts simultaneously
- Super-accurate internal GPS antenna
- StructureMap™, Broadband Radar™ and SIRIUS® weather overlay enhancements

Dominate with our easy-to-use touchscreen.

- Wide, super-bright 7-, 9- and 12-inch displays
- Customizable multi-panel views
- Intuitive, one-touch feature access
- Flexible networking with up to two Ethernet ports
- Performance upgrades including video camera input, SonicHub™ audio and more . . .

*PREVIEW THE **NEW** HDS GEN2 TOUCH AT...*

www.LOWRANCE.com/sws

Big Fish Don't Stand A Chance!

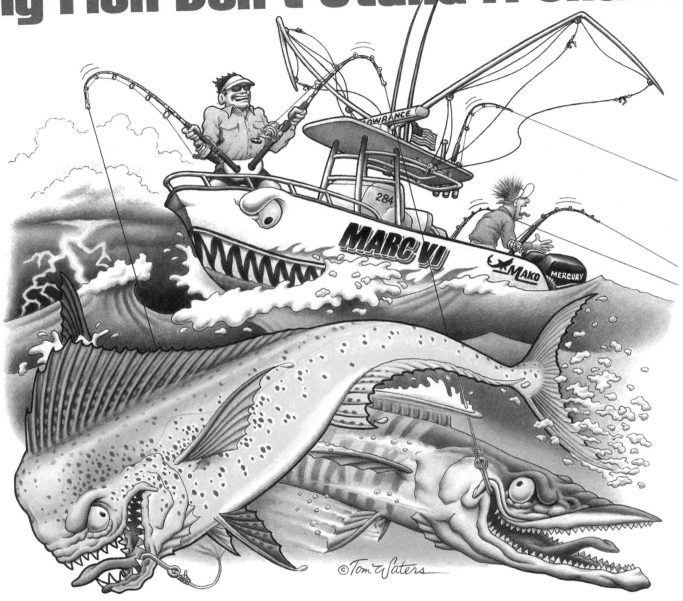

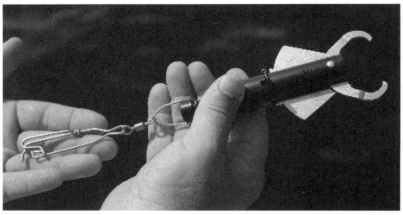

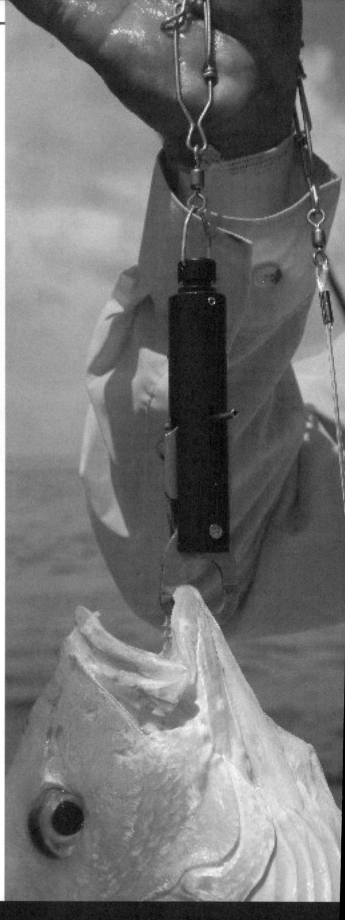

SeaQualizer is an innovative release tool designed to safely release bottom fish unharmed. With a changeable release setting of 50, 100, or 150ft the SeaQualizer simply attaches to the fish's jaw and pulls them back down to a safe release depth without having to "vent" the fish and possibly cause it more harm. Upon release, the device is then retrieved back to the boat either via rod and reel or on an attached release rope.

ICAST 2012
New Product Showcase WINNER

For more information visit us at **www.SeaQualizer.com**
or email us at **info@theseaqualizer.com**

NOTES

NOTES

NOTES